Development and Underdevelopment: A Marxist Analysis

GEOFFREY KAY

Lecturer in Economics
The City University, London

D0755469

First edition 1975
Reprinted 1975, 1976, 1977

Published by
THE MACMILLAN PRESS LTD

Associated companies in Delhi
Dublin Hong Kong Johannesburg Lagos
Melbourne New York Singapore Tokyo

ISBN 0 333 15402 9 (hardcover)
ISBN 0 333 21297 5 (paperback)

Printed and bound in Great Britain by
REDWOOD BURN LIMITED
Trowbridge & Esher

TO
ROGER GENOUD
STEPHEN HYMER
ROBERT SERESWESKI

Contents

Preface

Since 1968, the myth that *Capital* is unreadable has been exploded. Marxist literature, including Marx's own writings, now proliferate as never before. This recrudescence has a real basis in developments during the sixties: the collapse of consensus politics; the decomposition of the affluent society and the failure of the Americans to win a decisive victory in Vietnam. It also has ideological roots, for as the world has moved on academic social science has stood still.

Economics is no exception. Faced with developments they cannot grasp, the economists have retreated behind a veil of obscurantism and statistics vainly hoping that by measuring and correlating the appearance of effects they will get some clue as to causes. As their conventional orthodoxy, neo-classical theory, has collapsed under the weight of its own internal inconsistencies, economists have desperately appropriated terms and methods from the natural sciences in the hope that this guise of science might be mistaken for the real thing. Some students may be taken in by it, but many are bored and frustrated. Those students who turn to economics in the hope of finding some explanation of the developments they see around them: developments such as rising affluence and increasing stringency; growing wealth and grinding poverty; not to mention urban decay, pollution and underdevelopment – developments, in short, which threaten the very existence of civilisation: these students are still taught the key to analysis lies in understanding the way an isolated individual chooses whether to buy an overcoat or spaghetti.

The study of underdevelopment, it is true, has always been broader than that of other problems, and even orthodox development economists have been forced to take other so-called non-economic factors into account and recognise a historical dimension. But this has only highlighted their ideological prejudices. As I argue in the Introduction, orthodox development theory was never more than elaborate apology for

colonialism, and for this reason quickly came under attack from
the supporters of the nationalist movements that spread so
rapidly around the underdeveloped world. This criticism was
soon generalised against an even more fundamental proposition of orthodox theory, that underdevelopment was an original
condition for which capitalism could not be held responsible.
By the mid-sixties a whole school of radical development
economists had emerged which held the opposite view. Glaring
inconsistencies in orthodox theory were brought to light and
historical studies were produced to show how important
capitalist penetration had been. But this is as far as it went.
As none of the major works produced by this school was firmly
based on the *law of value* which Marx discovered and elaborated,
little progress could be made beyond this point. The radical
critics of orthodox development theory were so keen to prove
the ideological point that underdevelopment was the product
of capitalist exploitation, that they let the crucial issue pass
them by: capital created underdevelopment not because it exploited the underdeveloped world, but because it did not
exploit it enough.

I have written this book with the intention that it should be
understandable to readers with no previous knowledge of
Marxism or economics. The opening chapters consist of an
introduction to Marx's economic thought and all the concepts
that are subsequently used in the later chapters are explained
sufficiently for even the technical sections of chapters 5 and 6,
which contain the heart of my argument to be followed. If this
work achieves its goal of comprehensibility without compromise
to the complexity of its subject, much of the credit must go to
Susan Bennett who took the time and trouble to work through
it with me on a line by line basis. I should also like to thank
Antonio Bronda, Charmian Campbell, Peter Cusack, Feruccio
Gambino, Alex Macdonald, John Merrington, Roger Murray
and Ian and Beryl Tolady for their intellectual and moral
support. My colleagues at The City University eased my teach-
ing load at a crucial time and Marian White and Mary Keane
worked wonders with a ragged manuscript.

GEOFFREY KAY

The City University, London,
December 1973

Introduction

The concepts, development and underdevelopment, have only been widely used in their present sense since the end of the Second World War. For most of modern history the economic and social divisions of the world were understood as expressions of natural differences in race and climate. Differences in income were treated in much the same way as differences, say, in rainfall, and as late as 1930 a senior British administrator could blandly comment that average *per capita* income of £30 in Ghana compared not unfavourably with £80 in Britain.[1] In the colonial mind the world was divided into civilised men and natives and the gulf that divided them was considered unbridgeable – at least in the foreseeable future. Attitudes have now changed, and the view of the world embodied in the concepts of development and underdevelopment no longer holds the division to be permanent and fixed. Underdevelopment implies development in a way that barbarism never implied civilisation. The differences between an underdeveloped country and a developed one are of degree rather than kind; and the very use of these terms suggests that they are differences that can and should be overcome. It is, to say the least, a more positive outlook.

The immediate explanation for this radical departure in thought is the rise of nationalism in most parts of the underdeveloped world after 1945. For national sovereignty can have no real meaning unless it is joined to the idea of development as progress towards a social and economic equality from which no nation is debarred for natural reasons. National sovereignty and development defined in this way adhere to each other as closely as the principle of equal rights adheres to that of the freedom of the individual. In fact they can be correctly interpreted as a projection of these eighteenth-century principles on to an international stage. In this sense contemporary

[1] A. W. Cardinal, *The Gold Court, 1931* (Accra; Government Printer, 1931).

nationalism and economic development reveal their historical pedigree quite clearly as the latest episode in a drama which started two hundred years ago with the American and French revolutions. But the drama no longer carries conviction. Just as the principles of freedom and equality were emasculated in the nineteenth century and reduced to hollow, formal and reactionary incantations, so nationalist cries and the demand for development have been drained of whatever revolutionary content they may once have possessed.

The innate conservatism of development in practice, though hidden from view in the early years after the Second World War, was always apparent in the body of economic theory that grew up about it. Conventional development economics, in particular, has never been more than a thinly veiled apology for colonialism. Its formal commitment to nationalist aspirations for economic parity with the developed countries has always been outweighed by the implications of its basic concept of *original underdevelopment*. For if underdevelopment is an original condition in the way that conventional development economists assume; if it is a condition in which all countries once existed (characterised by such things as poverty, low labour productivity, backward technology, inadequate equipment and a heavy dependence upon a primitive agrarian sector), then the responsibility for its creation cannot be attributed to any class or country.[2] Colonialism is exonerated. While the more liberal development economist might concede that particular colonial governments did not do everything in their power to speed progress in the colonies, the point remains that his theoretical premises preclude him from even considering colonialism as a dimension of the problem. In fact, they preclude him from seriously examining underdevelopment as

[2] The term *original* or *traditional* underdevelopment was coined by Gunder Frank to characterise orthodox development theory which he criticised so severely. See A. G. Frank, *Capitalism and Underdevelopment in Latin America* (New York and London; Monthly Review Press, 1967), p. 3. His criticisms, although never satisfactorily refuted, have not prevented the authors of a recent textbook from asserting that 'underdevelopment . . . has been the normal state of all human societies apart from the few which, in the last two centuries, have applied a scientific technology to production and warfare'. Joan Robinson and Joan Eatwell, *An Introduction to Modern Economics* (London; McGraw-Hill, 1973), p. 323.

a historical process with particular social, economic and political co-ordinates. In the last analysis, conventional development economics does no more than reaffirm the colonial view that underdevelopment is a natural phenomenon, though the mood of the times no longer allowed this view to be stated in terms of racial differences and explained by the laws of social Darwinism. Since 1945, prejudice has had to change its 'scientific' language.

The first reason for this conservative bias was the cold war. As a result of war-time experience when communists had played a leading role in anti-fascist and anti-Nazi liberation movements and had in fact seized state power in some countries – China and Yugoslavia – and had only been prevented from doing the same in others by massive economic and military intervention – Greece, Turkey, Korea, Indo-China and even France and Italy – it is hardly surprising that the nationalist movements in the underdeveloped world were viewed with suspicion in the West. Nor is it too surprising that these suspicions should have been communicated to academic economists working in the field of development. This does not mean that they were part of a conspiracy, or, for that matter, even aware of the political ends their work subserved. It is true that one of the leading contributors in this area seized the bull by the horns and declared his work a *non-communist manifesto*,[3] but the majority denied all political motivation and genuinely believed in their scientific impartiality. But, if anything, this strengthened rather than weakened their ideological effectiveness. Who can claim impartiality and scientific objectivity more effectively than one who really does believe himself impartial? What better critic of radical nationalism could be found than the objective scientist – the expert?

However, one cannot prove a theory wrong simply by pointing to its political co-ordinates. Any criticism which does not tackle the scientific credentials of a theory directly can never be more than ideological. A theory is not necessarily incorrect just because the man who expounds it works for the United States government. A complete criticism must go further. In this case it must attack the second major influence on

[3] W. W. Rostow, *The Stages of Economic Growth* (London; Cambridge University Press, 1960).

conventional development economics – the body of theory which provides the real basis for its scientific pretensions – *neo-classical economics.*

As a coherent body of economic thought neo-classicism emerged in the late nineteenth century, though many of its elements can be traced back much earlier. Since this time it has dominated academic economics: most contemporary text-books are firmly situated within its framework and the majority of economists today still regard it as the only form of economics to have serious content or scientific status. It is possible to restrict the definition of neo-classicism to particular theories and methods of analysis. But it is also possible to characterise it as a general approach to economics and society at large, and it is in these broad terms we shall discuss it.[4] Its main distinguishing features can be summarised as follows:

(1) It asserts the existence of a universal economic problem, *scarcity*, which is unaffected by history in the sense that it is the common feature of every form of society – slave, feudal, capitalist, socialist. In all societies means fall short of ends, since wants are assumed unlimited by nature while the means by which they can be satisfied are always limited by definition. Thus neo-classical economics, which defines its object of study as the allocation of scarce means to unlimited ends, is inevitably *ahistorical.*

(2) It is predicated upon a perspective of *social harmony* and while it acknowledges that conflicts can arise in practice, it believes them to be transitory in principle and contingent by nature.

(3) It indentifies three factors of production – land (including raw materials), labour and capital (usually defined as

---

[4] Taken in these broad terms it corresponds closely to what Marx called *vulgar economy*. In contradistinction to political economy which 'has investigated the real relations of production in bourgeois society . . . vulgar economy . . . deals with appearances only, ruminates ceaselessly on materials long since provided by scientific economy, and there seeks explanations from the most obtrusive phenomena, for bourgeois daily use, but for the rest, confines itself to systematising in a pedantic way, and proclaiming for ever-lasting truths, trite ideas held by the self-complacent bourgeoisie with regard to their own world, to them the best of all possible worlds'. Karl Marx, *Capital*, vol. 1, 3rd ed. (George Allen and Unwin), p. 53.

machinery and equipment) – which are all *materially* indispensable for production. It then asserts that these factors are *socially* equivalent to each other. Although there are different streams of thought on this question, the common position is that the owners of these factors are rewarded in the form of rent, wages and profits respectively, according to what they contribute to the value of production. This excludes any possibility of exploitation: if everyone is paid according to his contribution to the value of the social product, no matter what form this contribution might take, then no one can gain anything which is not properly his. At a stroke any real basis for exploitation and class struggle is removed.

(4) Although it has no adequate concepts for distinguishing capitalist society from any other form of society, neo-classical economics takes the traditional property relations of capitalism as universal and desirable. It worships at the shrine of private property.

Conventional development economics reproduces all this faithfully. Its assertion that the developed countries are in no fundamental way responsible for underdevelopment parallels the neo-classical assertion that capital does not exploit labour; its moralistic injunction to all countries to work together in their common interest is an extrapolation of the theory of social harmony on to the international scale. But neo-classical economics has shaped contemporary development theory in an even more important way which has helped it to survive and even absorb a great deal of the radical criticism levelled against it in recent years.

If we had to single out one of the four features of neo-classicism just listed as the most fundamental, it would certainly be the first. The ideological nature of neo-classicism is more apparent in the other three, but it is this one that determines its method of analysis and thus predetermines all its findings. Its definition of the economic problem as one of scarcity turns neo-classical economics into an exclusively *quantitative* analysis. It directs attention to such questions as: How much does a country produce? What is the level of *per capita* income? and so on. Other questions such as those that concern the social relations that men enter into when they engage in economic activity – relations of master and slave; lord and serf; capitalist and wage-labourer – simply do not figure and can be dismissed as irrelevant.[5] Or rather they can be left out of account in the first instance and then introduced later by a sleight of hand to fix an ideological point. Development economics offers us a clear example of how this is done.

The analysis begins by distinguishing development from underdevelopment with the use of some purely quantitative indicator such as income per head. Individual underdeveloped economies are then examined and it is invariably found that according to this measure the economy has two sectors: one where income is high and the other where it is low. The high-income sector is then seen as the developing or modern sector; the low-income one as the underdeveloped or traditional sector. For good measure the two are then considered to be separate from each other, so the problem of development can be defined as discovering means to transfer labour and resources from the second to the first.[6] The *coup de grâce* is then to call the developing sector capitalist, which is invariably true,

---

[5] Alfred Marshall, one of the founders of neo-classical economics, concludes the second paragraph of his major work with an eloquent statement on the importance of the social aspect of production. 'For the business by which a person earns his livelihood generally fills his thoughts during by far the greater part of those hours in which his mind is at its best; during these hours his character is being formed by the way in which he uses his faculties in his work, by the thoughts and feelings which it suggests, and by his relations to his associates in work, his employers or his employees'. But straight away he adds: 'the influence exerted on a person's character by the amount of his income is hardly less, if it is less, than that exerted by the way in which it is earned', and this is the line he pursues with few deviations through the next 700 pages. Alfred Marshall, *Principles of Economics*, 8th ed. (London; Macmillan, 1920), p. 1.

[6] Here, in essence, we have *the theory of the dual economy*, which rests upon the simple proposition that the rate of economic growth (i.e. development) is determined by the interaction of the rate of savings and the capital-output ratio. As the latter is invariably assumed constant, everything depends upon the former. By the use of reductionist logic this is assumed to depend upon the level of average *per capita* income. Thus in the underdeveloped sector of an economy, where income is low, savings, and consequently growth, are low, while in the developing sector, income is high, savings are plentiful and growth is self-sustaining. This theory of underdevelopment, as a vicious circle of poverty, of course, precludes development even as a possibility, for if underdevelopment by its very nature reproduces underdevelopment, it

and the underdeveloped sector non-capitalist which is altogether a more ambiguous proposition. For what this labelling does without any justification whatsoever is to identify development with capitalism and underdevelopment with non-capitalism. Although development economics is set up in such a way as to preclude even considering capitalism as a cause of underdevelopment, it is able by playing about with definitions in this way to confidently assert that capitalism is the source of development.

To make matters more complicated this assertion happens to be right. Capitalism is indeed the source of development according to every accepted definition of that term. But the neo-classical economist, unable to distinguish capitalism from any other mode of production, cannot claim any scientific basis for this conclusion. However, as it is always more difficult to disprove a theory which gives the right answers, so to speak, than one that gives wrong answers, most of the criticism directed against development theory has attacked the other side of its argument. It has set about demonstrating the claim that capitalism is not responsible for underdevelopment to be false.[7] And although much valuable work has been done to this end – work which can be said to have cracked the subject open – ultimately it has led up a blind alley.

Firstly, leading circles in the advanced capitalist countries themselves have proved willing to accept, tacitly at least, that capitalism and colonialism were responsible for under-development.[8] As the cold war receded in the sixties and the threat

---

is incapable of generating development. So how does the orthodox development economist explain such concrete phenomena as the industrial revolution in Britain? Rostow, whose whole work finally stands or falls by his ability to analyse what he calls the British take-off, offers us the following penetrating insight '. . . only in Britain were the necessary and sufficient conditions fulfilled. This combination of necessary and sufficient conditions for a take-off was the result of a convergence of a number of quite independent circumstances, a kind of statistical accident of history . . .' Rostow, *The Stages of Economic Growth*, p. 31.

[7] The most swingeing critique to date is surely that of A. G. Frank, *Sociology of Development* (London; Pluto Press, 1971).

[8] As early as 1922, the advance guards of the capitalist class were looking to the future. 'When the natives of Africa begin raising their own cotton and the natives of Russia begin making their own farming implements and

of international communism posed by the Soviet Union weakened, the matter lost much of its immediate political importance. Moreover, making abstract concessions about the past is a good way of winning real concessions for the future, and it occurred to the more far-sighted circles in the Western world that admissions of past faults backed up by assurances of good behaviour in the future provided a sound basis for understanding with new nationalist governments. Just as the most ardent supporter of capitalism today would be prepared to admit that capitalism was in large measure responsible for the appalling conditions in the nineteenth-century factories, emphasising, of course, just how much matters have changed since then: so the far-sighted Western statesman today is prepared to admit many failures in the past, so long, of course, as attention is fixed firmly on the future. At the same time those powerful elements in the nationalist movement which were never anti-capitalist even from the start, found this criticism of capitalism and its tacit acceptance in the West very much to their liking, for it gave them every opportunity to adopt a radical posture which meant almost nothing in practice. In short, by the time the radical criticism was elaborated in the sixties it had lost most of its political force and could evoke little more than moral protest.

Secondly, the claim that capitalism played no role in the creation of underdevelopment is so blatantly false that it could be easily disproved on empirical grounds alone without any far-reaching theoretical criticism of development economics and its neo-classical under-pinnings.[9] This exposed the criticism to a conservative reabsorption and there grew up a new ortho-

---

the natives of China begin making their own wants, it will make a difference, to be sure, but does any thoughtful man imagine that the world can continue on the present basis of a few nations supplying the needs of the world? We must think in terms of what the world will be when civilisation (i.e. industrial capitalism) becomes general, when all peoples have learned to help themselves'. Henry Ford, *My Life and Work* (London: William Heinemann Ltd., 1922), p. 243.

[9] Thus Keith Griffin, for example, has launched a devastating empirical attack against orthodox development economics without really challenging its theoretical premises. See Keith Griffin, *Underdevelopment in Spanish America* (London: George Allen and Unwin, 1969), especially the introduction.

doxy known as *structuralist economics*.[10] Protagonists of this
new school of thought explained underdevelopment in terms
of the manner in which the colonies and neo-colonies of the
nineteenth century had been integrated into the world economy
by the advanced capitalist nations, and turned into suppliers
of primary commodities and importers of manufactured goods.
The structure of production and consumption became dis-
located as a result, with underdeveloped countries producing
goods they never used and using goods they could not produce.
Their progress came to depend entirely upon being able to balance their foreign trade. If they could not sell their exports in
sufficient quantity they would be unable to buy from the developed countries machinery and equipment to create new industries and jobs. In this way the problems of under-development

[10] Many of the important contributions in this field are to be found in
four collections of essays: *The Economics of Underdevelopment*, ed. A. N.
Agarwala and S. P. Singh (London: Oxford University Press, 1958);
Imperialism and Underdevelopment, a reader, ed. Robert I. Rhodes (New York
and London: Monthly Review Press, 1970); ed. Roger Owen and Bob
Sutcliffe. *Studies in the Theory of Imperialism* (London: Longman, 1972);
Underdevelopment and Development; ed. Henry Bernstein, (London: Penguin
Books, 1973). See also Paul A. Baran, *The Political Economy of Growth*,
Monthly Review 1957, (London: Penguin Books, 1973); also Celso Furtado,
Development and Underdevelopment (Berkeley and Los Angeles: University of
California Press, 1964); H. Myint, *The Economics of Developing Countries*
(London: Hutchinson University Library, 1964); F. A. Clairmonte, *Eco-
nomic Liberalism and Underdevelopment* (Bombay: Asia Publishing House, 1960).
The uniting theme of these works is their effort to explain the process of
underdevelopment in terms of the *dependence* of underdeveloped countries
upon developed countries. Gunder Frank has stated this theme in the most
general and radical terms: 'As a photograph of the world taken at a point
in time, this model consists of a world metropolis (today the United States)
and its governing class, and its national and international satellites and
their leaders – national satellites like the Southern States of the United
States, and international satellites like Sao Paulo. Since Sao Paulo is a
national metropolis in its own right, the model consists further of its satellites; the provincial metropolises, like Recife or Belo Horizonte, and their
regional and local satellites in turn. That is, taking a photograph of a slice
of the world we get a whole chain of metropolises and satellites which runs
from the world metropolis down to the hacienda or rural merchant who
are satellites of the local commercial metropolitan centre but who in turn
have peasants as their satellites. If we take a photograph of the world as a
whole, we get a whole series of such constellations of metropolises and
satellites. The form of this metropolis-satellite relationship changes historically'. See Frank, *Capitalism and Underdevelopment*, pp. 146–7.

were redefined in terms of trade relations with the developed countries who were enjoined to offer favourable concessions. But the matter was still conceived in an essentially quantitative fashion and this prevented any effective criticism of the relations of production that lay at the heart of the problem. The theory lacked a revolutionary political dimension. As their criticism did not attack the neo-classical basis of development theory directly, radical structuralists were forced to import their political positions in exactly the same way as neo-classicism, even though the positions were different. They were never able to go beyond revolutionary phraseology.

But given the revolutionary positions that were adopted, it might appear surprising, at first sight, that so few attempts were made to use Marx's work except for the occasional quotation. Certainly no radical work in the field throughout the fifties and for much of the sixties even sought to base itself directly on the *law of value* as elaborated by Marx in *Capital*. One explanation is that Stalinism so appalled the liberal inclinations of the radical elements in the West, that they tended to turn them away from Marxism altogether. The heavy anti-Marxist ideology of the cold war is another. But by the mid-sixties both these pressures had weakened and a new generation of left-wing intellectuals had emerged opposed to the war in Vietnam and with a direct experience of the convulsions of 1968. The way was open to a new Marxist interpretation of development and underdevelopment, except for one major obstacle which has proved very hard to overcome. Classical Marxist writings do not appear to have very much to say on the subject, as the problem of underdevelopment was scarcely foreseen let alone analysed in the nineteenth century.[11] In fact, the few passages in the main caucus of Marxist theory which deal directly with the spread of capitalism throughout the world appeared to anticipate not underdevelopment but development. For example, in the *Communist Manifesto* Marx and Engels established this perspective:

> The bourgeoisie, by the rapid development of all instruments of production, by the immensely facilitated means of com-

[11] See Sutcliffe, 'Imperialism and Industrialisation in the Third World', in *Studies in the Theory of Imperialism*, ed. Owen and Sutcliffe, especially pp. 180–5.

munication, draws all, even the most barbarian nations into civilisation. The cheap prices of its commodities are the heavy artillery with which it batters down all Chinese walls, with which it forces the barbarians' intensely obstinate hatred of foreigners to capitulate. It compels all nations, on pain of extinction, to adopt the bourgeois mode of production; it compels them to introduce what it calls civilisation into their midst – i.e. they become bourgeois themselves. In one word, it creates a world after its own image.[12]

Five years later, in 1853, in an article on the 'Future Results of British Rule in India', Marx expressed the same view in more concrete terms:

I know that the English millocracy intend to endow India with railways with the exclusive view of extracting at diminished expense the cotton and other raw materials for their manufacture. But when you have once introduced machinery into the locomotion of a country, which possesses iron and coals, you are unable to withhold it from its fabrication. You cannot maintain a net of railways over an immense country without introducing all those industrial processes necessary to meet the immediate and current wants of railway locomotion, and out of which there must grow the application of machinery to those branches of industry not immediately connected with railways. The railway-system will therefore become, in India, truly, the forerunner of modern industry.[13]

And in 1867, in the preface to the first edition of *Capital*, there occurs the famous statement:

The country that is more developed industrially only shows, to the less developed, the image of its own future.[14]

A similar view is adopted by Lenin in his work on imperialism.

[12] Marx and Engels, '*The Communist Manifesto*', in Karl Marx, *The Revolutions of 1848*, edited and introduced by David Fernbach (London: Penguin Books in association with New Left Review, 1973), p. 71.
[13] Marx, '*The Future Results of British Rule in India*', in Karl Marx, *Surveys from Exile*, edited and introduced by David Fernbach (London, Penguin Books in association with New Left Review, 1973), pp. 323–4.
[14] Marx, *Capital*, vol. 1, p. xvii.

The export of capital influences, greatly accelerates, the development of capitalism in those countries to which it is exported. While, therefore, the export of capital may tend to a certain extent to arrest development in the capital exporting countries, it can only do so by expanding and deepening the further development of capitalism throughout the world.[15]

It would be absurd to claim that a few passages such as these have been responsible in themselves for delaying the production of a theory of underdevelopment based upon the *law of value*, or that their mere existence makes the production of such a theory impossible. Nevertheless, in so far as its general historical perspective is that the historical role of capitalism is to develop men's productive forces to a hitherto unprecedented extent, Marxist theory is difficult to reconcile with the existence of worldwide underdevelopment brought about by capitalism. But not impossible. On the contrary, the law of value provides the only satisfactory basis for such a theory which is not only adequate to its object, but which is also the definitive critique both scientifically and politically of conventional development theory and its radical offshoots.

[15] V. I. Lenin, *Imperialism, The Highest Stage of Capitalism*, (Moscow: Foreign Languages Publishing House), p. 107.

1 Production, Consumption and Surplus

All societies, whether primitive or advanced, contemporary or of the past, must reproduce themselves from one year to the next. They must maintain their population and replenish their physical stocks. This requires that they engage in the process of *material production*. Material production is, therefore, the common feature of all societies. In a real sense it is the starting point of society itself, and for this reason it provides a starting point for economic theory.[1]

The essence of material production consists of the actions men take upon nature in their effort to humanise it; its aim is to transform natural objects of little or no use in their original form into a condition where they can satisfy human needs. Hollowing out a tree to make a canoe is a simple example;

[1] Material production is the point at which Marx started his analysis in the Introduction to the *Grundrisse*, but as Martin Nicolaus explains it was a starting point that left Marx dissatisfied. The reasons for this are extremely complex, for they involve the very essence of dialetical materialism. The crux of the matter is that the category material production, and the related ones of consumption and distribution, are ahistorical because they apply to all societies: with their use, Marx observes, 'no real historical stage of production can be grasped'. In contradistinction the starting point of *Capital*, the commodity, and the categories that are imminent within it such as exchange value, abstract labour, money and capital itself, not only presuppose the general categories of material production (value) and consumption (use-value) but 'bear the stamp of history'. Definite historical conditions are necessary that a product may become a commodity' (*Capital, vol. 1*, p. 148). This does not mean that the theoretical analysis of commodities is a historical analysis in the sense of being an examination of the concrete conditions of commodity production and their actual development. The theory elaborated in *Capital* is historical only in so far as the categories it deploys are historically specific to the capitalist mode of production and are not applicable to any other form of society. See Marx, *Grundrisse* (Penguin Books, 1973), especially Martin Nicolaus's brilliant foreword, p. 35 *et seq*. Material production is taken as a starting point here with all its limitations in mind, partly for simplicity and partly because it allows the banalities of neo-classical economics which starts with the individual and exchange to be readily criticised in anticipation of what follows.

using iron, coal, tin, rubber and so on to manufacture a car is a more complex one: but in both cases the principle is the same. Both the canoe and the car are *products* as opposed to natural objects, since their existence depends upon human action – *labour*. We can therefore define a product as a natural object transformed by human labour so that it can satisfy a human need. This process of transformation is the process of material production.

One theme of history comprises changes in this process from forms of production where men do little more than respond to the dictates of nature, to others where they begin to understand natural processes and intervene in them with ever greater consciousness. Hunting and gathering are examples of the most primitive type of production, since the human producer is entirely dependent upon nature for the maturation of his product. For this reason they represent a lower level of development than organised agriculture, where the producers begin to intervene directly in the process of maturation, and, to the extent that their knowledge of natural laws has progressed, are able to exercise a measure of control over it. Agriculture of various levels of sophistication has historically been the most important form of productive activity that men have undertaken and it is only in the industrial countries in the comparatively recent past that it has ceased to occupy the vast majority of the labour force. If one takes employment as an indicator it is still far and away the most important type of material production undertaken in the underdeveloped world.

The increased knowledge with which men confront nature in the productive process expresses itself most immediately in the complexity of the means of production, particularly the tools and machines, they have at their disposal. These *instruments of labour* vary from the simplest spear of a primitive hunter to the most up-to-date automated machine systems. In modern manufacturing industry the instruments used by labour have become so vast and complex that they often appear to have a life and significance of their own. But this is deceptive. No matter how complex, all instruments of labour are products; they are the result of human labour and the technological knowledge they embody is human knowledge. Everyday experience in capitalist society suggests the opposite: it suggests that machines are active co-partners with labour in the process of production. But everyday experience and common sense are notoriously poor guides to the true nature of things. In capitalist society they mystify even the most basic concepts. When it is used as the basis for scientific analysis, as in economics, it even fails to distinguish people from inanimate objects.

1. *The law of social reproduction*

Material production is the starting point for all social existence since it provides the *means of consumption* – the food, the clothing, the shelter and so on – that enable a population to survive from one year to the next. Production makes possible consumption; but consumption is also necessary for production. For if the producers do not consume their basic essentials, they cannot survive and work. The two are therefore inseparable and we can analyse their interdependence by means of a circuit, $P\ldots C_n\ldots P\ldots$, where P represents production and C_n, consumption. The relationship defined in this circuit must exist in some form or other in all societies; in fact it is the most basic statement of the fundamental *law of social reproduction*.

Consumption, in the basic circuit of social reproduction, is restricted to *necessary consumption*, that is the amount of consumption necessary to maintain the existing level of production. In addition to the eventual consumption of the direct producers, it must include the wear and tear and depletion of the means of production as a result of their use. As production takes place tools and machines get worn down and stocks of materials get used up, and unless this depreciation is made good the level of social production cannot be maintained.

Necessary consumption, therefore, consists of two types of consumption: the *personal consumption* of the producers and the *productive consumption* of means of production. Personal consumption is so called because it refers to that which is necessary to the producers as living beings, and covers what they consume as persons: productive consumption indicates the material objects used up, i.e. consumed, in the process of production itself. For any society to reproduce itself from one year to the next, it is necessary that its level of social production should at least cover these two component parts of necessary consumption. But while the circuit of social reproduction must function in every society, its operations become less apparent in more advanced societies. In capitalist society, especially, it is so deeply submerged into the diverse forms of social and economic activity that characterise this type of society that it is invisible to the empirical eye. Its existence is hidden behind (1) the systematic production of a substantial *surplus* over the level of consumption necessary for simple reproduction; and (2) the existence of the *market*. The latter is far and away the most confusing and we can make no progress until we are clear about its fundamental nature and significance.

The real basis of the market, and indeed of the surplus, is the *division of labour* which has advanced in capitalist society far beyond anything previously attained. Production has been broken down into a vast array of separate activities organised by an army of individual enterprises scattered over the whole world, in comparison to which all earlier forms of production appear parochial. Producers are separated from each other as producers and further separated from themselves as consumers. Production for immediate use plays no part in this order, and there are few items of consumption whose origins cannot be traced back through several branches of production, frequently sited in different countries. Thus, for instance, a host of intermediaries intervene between the consumer of a loaf and the farmer who grows the wheat; moreover, except for those occasional farmers who bake for themselves, the same intermediaries intervene between farmers as producers of wheat and farmers as consumers of bread. As a consequence of this unparalleled articulation of the division of labour, the basic circuit of social reproduction has itself become exceptionally complex, and requires highly specialised mechanisms to ensure its operations. The mechanisms that serve this purpose and through which the circuit of social reproduction is organised in capitalist society are known collectively as the market. Although most of the elements of the market, including money, preceded the emergence of capitalism, it is only in capitalist society that the market becomes fully developed and embraces all aspects of economic and social life.

In this form of society the circuit of social reproduction

operates through the market, which replaces the more direct links of earlier forms of society where producers and consumers lived in a much closer relationship to each other. In a feudal manor or tribal village where the division of labour extended over proportionately very few people, and the vast majority of the items of necessary consumption were produced within the framework of the collective, no special mechanisms for circulating and distributing products were necessary. These economic functions were performed through social, political and even religious institutions, although the way in which this happened varied considerably from one society to the next. The division of labour in capitalist society that separates producers from each other and from consumers to an unprecedented extent smashed these traditional forms of exchange. In their place has developed, in the form of the market, an economic institution, more specialised and more separated from other aspects of social existence, than any that has previously existed. As a result, economic relations between men assume the garb of market or *exchange* relations, and the main form of economic activity appears to be buying and selling. As a result, it often appears that the real basis of economic activity consists of the inter-relationship of supply and demand rather than production and consumption. But any analysis based on this approach must lead up a cul-de-sac, for it is based upon a fundamental error. The organisation of the links between production and consumption, no matter how complicated they might be, can never, either in theory or in practice, take precedence over production and consumption themselves. Organisation is always secondary to what is being organised. Despite its indispensability to the capitalist economy the market is always subordinate to the real activities of production and consumption.

These activities determine market relations (i.e. the supply and demand of different products and their relative prices) and not vice versa. The law of social reproduction requires that part of the social product consists of items of necessary personal consumption for the producers, who, in capitalist society, are wage-labourers, since their continued survival and capacity to produce is the first condition for the continued existence of the society as a whole. Further, the law of social reproduction determines the relative prices of these products taken together as a general category in relation to money wages and imposes them upon the market. To show why this is the case we must anticipate a part of our argument and briefly consider the nature of the *wage.*

All economists agree that the wage is a price like any other, in the sense that it is a payment for something that is sold. It is the price that an employer pays to a worker in return for work he performs. The sum of all wages paid in an economy then equals the total payment made by all employers as a class to all workers as a class. Moreover, this payment is made in the form of money, so that at the end of the week the working class finds itself in possession of a certain sum of cash, which it can use to buy the products offered for sale on the market. While each individual worker can exercise a measure of discretion over his choice of what to buy, the law of social reproduction dictates that each worker and his family purchase sufficient products of a type that satisfy the needs of necessary personal consumption. For this to be possible, it is obvious that the sum of money wages must at least equal the sum of the prices of items of necessary personal consumption taken as a whole. In other words the law of social reproduction determines the lower limit to one of the most crucial price ratios in the economy, the ratio between the money wage and the prices of essential consumer goods taken as a category; and it does quite independently of market forces. In fact, this limit is imposed on the market, not established by it.

The upper limit to this ratio is determined in an identical way. If the total money value of wages equalled the market price of all products so that the working class could buy everything that was produced, nothing would be left to make good the productive consumption. In other words, the law of social reproduction dictates that while the wage must be sufficiently high to allow the working class as a whole to buy its means of necessary consumption, it must leave a sufficient amount of the social product over to cover productive consumption. Nor is this all. If the whole social product except for productive consumption could be purchased by the working class with its wages, nothing would be left over for their employers to get as profits. Since employers readily admit that their main concern is profits, and but for profits there would be no reason for them to go into business, profits are as essential to production in this type of society as necessary consumption.

To summarise: the law of social reproduction as it operates in capitalist society determines a number of crucial price ratios in the economy and imposes them on the market. Supply and demand reflect these imperatives: production and consumption determine supply and demand and relative prices. We must be clear about the nature of this determination. The law of social reproduction determines the ratio of the money wage to the prices of products in a literal sense of setting limits to these ratios. The lower limit is that the money wage must be sufficient to allow the working class to purchase its items of necessary personal consumption; the upper limit must leave part of the social product over to cover productive consumption and profits. These limits can vary marginally from year to year, but are more or less fixed in the long run. The market can only operate freely within them: it cannot override them. In practice this will allow considerable scope to the autonomous operation of market forces: on the other hand to concentrate on this autonomy without first specifying its limits must lead to a profound misunderstanding of the role of the market in the capitalist economy.[2] Thus, our first conclusion is that the most important thing about supply and demand and prices is that they are not as important as all that.

2. *The circuit of production and consumption*

We must now examine the relationship between production and consumption more closely. In the circuit of social reproduction, $P \ldots C_n \ldots P \ldots$, the two are entirely interdependent:

---

[2] Where an essential need such as that, say, for protein, can be satisfied in different ways, by different forms of food, say meat and nuts, the law of social reproduction does not affect relative prices directly in so far as its conditions can be satisfied by any combination of the production and consumption of the two commodities, subject, of course, to the constraint that the total production and consumption of both is sufficient. But this condition is lost sight of if attention is focussed exclusively upon the proportion in which the items are produced and consumed. Moreover, if the factors that determine this proportion are made the starting point of analysis, as neoclassical economics makes them, the illusion is created that production and consumption are free of all social constraints and that they are determined by individual choices for particular products.

neither can take place without the other. But the connection between them is even closer: not only are production and necessary consumption inseparable in reality, but production, and consumption generally, are inseparable theoretically. Production implies consumption and vice versa in such a way that neither is *conceivable* without the other. For instance, it is impossible to develop a definition of production which does not imply consumption, as even our rudimentary definition of material production shows. In that definition it was necessary to point out that the end of production, the product, must satisfy a human need and serve as an item of consumption.[3] Similarly, consumption implies production and we are drawn inescapably to the conclusion that the two are inseparable.[4] On the other hand they are not identical: production is quite distinct from consumption. In contemporary society this distinction is institutionalised through the division of time into work and leisure and of situation into factory and home.

Thus, even apparently simple and elementary concepts like the basic ones of production and consumption are exceedingly complex. The relationship between them is intricate and frequently its various strands contradict each other. Unfortunately, these difficulties cannot be ignored since they are a necessary reflection of the complex reality they are used to

[3] 'Because a product only becomes a real product through consumption. For example a dress becomes really a dress only by being worn, a house which is uninhabited is indeed not really a house. . . . It is evident that externally production supplies the object of consumption, it is evident that consumption posits the object of production . . .' Marx, 'Introduction to *Grundrisse*', from translation in *A Contribution to the Critique of Political Economy* (London: Lawrence and Wishart, 1971), pp. 196–7. In the language of commodities: 'nothing can have value without being an object of utility. If the thing is useless, so is the labour contained in it . . .' (*Capital*, vol. 1, p. 8).

[4] For this reason both appear equivalent and within the framework of this approach neither can be seen as more important than the other in determining social development. This is only another way in which the ahistorical generality of the concept of material production as a starting point of analysis reveals itself. On the other hand it does have the merit of showing how vacuous is the neo-classical approach where consumption is considered as the end of production and people *chose* to go out to work in order to consume.

clarify. One important point about this reality is the inter-connectedness of all different phenomena. An approach which concentrates upon this interconnectedness is totally opposed to that more current one, which defines concepts in a simple, one-dimensional fashion and sees the world in terms of a series of discreet and separate problems. Strikes, unemployment, pollution, underdevelopment, to name a few such 'problems', must inevitably be thought of in isolation if the concepts through which they are analysed are themselves defined in isolation from each other. But if we adopt a framework in which the concepts are defined in relation to each other, we automatically reject this approach in favour of another which treats phenomena as expressions of a complex and total structure. The way in which the basic concepts of a theory are set up – here the concepts are production and consumption – is vitally important, since it determines the general theoretical approach adopted and can largely pre-empt the conclusions it reaches.

3. *The social relations of production*

We must now further complicate our definition of production and consumption by recognising that they are not purely material activities. Each has a social dimension. Non-material factors such as religious taboos can determine whether or not a product can act as a means of consumption. For example, pork does not serve as food in Moslem or Jewish society. The social dimension of production arises from the fact that when men engage in this activity they not only involve themselves in a relationship with nature, i.e. material production, but they also enter into relationships with each other. These relationships are the *social relations of production* and they interact with material production in the same complex way that production in general interacts with consumption.

The nature of these social relations of production can be most readily appreciated from the way in which they affect the direct producer who is immediately responsible for the appropriation of the product from nature. They are directly expressed in his rights with regard to his own labour, to the means of production with which he works, and to what he produces. These rights have changed many times over in the course of history. Where the direct producer is a *slave* as in the

British West Indies and the southern states of America from the seventeenth to the nineteenth centuries, they are non-existent. Not only does the slave have no property rights in the means of production or the product of his labour, he is even denied rights in his own labour. In contrast to this, the feudal *serf* had very definite rights. He had guaranteed access to the use of land; he frequently owned his instruments of labour, and he could always claim part of the product for his own use. On the other hand he had very definite obligations to his *seigneur* which he was forced to discharge either by yielding up a part of his crop, or by performing unpaid labour on seigneurial land, or, towards the end of the feudal epoch, through the payment of a cash rent.

The situation of the *wage-labourer*, the direct producer in capitalist society, differs yet again. In contradistinction to both serf and slave he is not legally tied to a single occupation, but, in principle, can change his job and his employer as he wishes. In other respects his conditions of labour bear a closer resemblance to those of the slave than the serf. He has no rights over the means of production or the product of his labour. On the other hand he is legally entitled to remuneration which he receives in the form of a wage.

The combination of the two aspects of production: production as a material process on the one side, and as a social process on the other, constitutes a *mode of production*. The two sets of social relations, serf and seigneur, wage-labourer and capitalist, and the different forms of material production they engender, make up the two modes of production, *feudalism* and *capitalism*. They differ fundamentally except in one respect: under both there must be a persistent surplus of material production over necessary consumption. In feudal society unless production had regularly exceeded what was necessary to sustain the servile class and replenish the means of production as they were used up, the seigneurial class could never even have existed let alone embarked upon costly wars and established religious foundations. And if the seigneurial class had been absent, the producers would not have worked as serfs, for the category serf is inseparable from that of seigneur and cannot exist without it. In short, feudal society itself could never have existed without a continuous surplus of material production over necessary consumption. The same condition holds true for capitalism. Here, the social product must sustain the working class and make good the depreciation of the means of production before the capitalists can gain any profits. If production did not exceed necessary consumption, the capitalist class could not exist, let alone accumulate capital, and without this class the producers would not exist as wage-labourers, for this category is insepar-able from that of capital. Thus, the regular production of a surplus is the first pre-condition for the existence of capitalism. It is the first pre-condition of all *class societies* where one group appropriates the surplus produced by another.

Thus, while the development of material production to a stage where the production of a surplus becomes an established feature of economic life underlies the social relations of produc-tion in class society, and, in this general sense, can be said to determine them, these social relations are no mere reflex of material production. The *social* division of labour whereby in one epoch some men are serfs and others seigneurs, and at another, some men are wage-labourers and others capitalists, is not a *technical* division of labour. It does not follow auto-matically and inevitably from the prevailing techniques of material production. It is true that some types of production are inconsistent with some social relations of production. For instance, the development of machine production on a large scale inevitably wipes out small independent cottage producers, as happened in the textile industry during the industrial revolu-tion in Britain. It is also inconceivable that production in a society based upon mass production for a consumer market, with freedom of choice between brands, could be anything other than capitalist. It is impossible to sell cars to slaves! On the other hand, the prevailing social relations of production limit technology no less forcibly. In the feudal epoch, for in-stance, it proved extremely difficult, sometimes impossible, to introduce more efficient scythes even though they would have lightened the labour of the serfs. The reason was their very efficiency, for by cutting the crops closer to the ground less would have been left over for gleanage, which was a widely established right of the serfs.

Capitalist society abounds with similarly clear examples of the social relations of production, and the relations of private property associated with them, determining the nature of the technology employed and the form of material production. The proliferation of the car is a case in point. The technical knowledge used to produce cars could be used equally well to produce other types of vehicles such as buses, which could form the basis of a transport system organised predominantly on a public basis. Moreover, such a system would in all probability be more efficient, particularly in large cities: it would be safer, cheaper and cleaner. Yet it would not correspond so closely to the relations of private property that exist in capitalist society, as the present system of transport based predominantly on the private car. Moreover, its very efficiency would reduce its profitability, for the vast reduction in the number of vehicles produced and purchased would certainly cut back the profits of the huge sections of industry engaged directly and indirectly in transport. In other branches of the economy it is no less true that the social relations of production and the property relations arising from them, within which consumption takes place, determine the nature of material production. The decisions concerning what techniques to employ and what products to produce in capitalist society are limited by the fact that production is for profit and the majority of products are destined for private ownership. Other relations of production and property would yield different material results.

Again, we cannot escape the complexity of the problem. On the one hand material production determines the social relations within which it takes place; on the other these social relations determine material production no less forcibly. We must accept this complexity and work with it. It does not arise abstractly in the minds of those who seek to explain reality: on the contrary it arises out of reality. Complicated though it may be, it is simple in comparison with what it seeks to make understandable.

We can summarise the main arguments of this chapter in the form of three conditions which any theory which seeks to explain the law of social reproduction in the specific conditions of capitalist society must satisfy. (1) It must take account of the twofold nature of production as a material process on the one hand and as a social process on the other. (2) It must recognise the central role of the market as the mechanism of distribution and exchange, but at the same time show how this mechanism is subordinate to the real activities of production and consumption. (3) It must define its concepts in relation to each other in order to show the interconnectedness of all social and economic phenomena.

2 Surplus Value and Profit

The theory of surplus value explains how social reproduction takes place in the special situation of capitalist society. Its basic premises, unlike those of any other economic theory, satisfy all the conditions just laid down.

1. *Commodity and value*

Let us start with the *commodity*. In the first place this is a product. It is a natural object transformed by human labour into a form which satisfies some human need. It is a *use-value*. The nature of the use it serves is of secondary importance for a commodity exists as a use-value irrespective of the purpose to which it is put. Thus, food which satisfies a biological need is qualitatively completely different from, say, musical instruments which can satisfy an aesthetic need. But both are use-values because they satisfy a need.

The vast majority of products in capitalist society are not consumed directly by those who produce them. In other words very few products serve as use-values for their direct producers. As we have seen, this arises from the highly developed division of labour which is characteristic of capitalist society, and without which it could not exist. Moreover, as we remarked in the last chapter, the articulation of the division of labour has provided the real basis for the development of the market. It is the market that provides the link between production and consumption in capitalist society, and the number of products in this form of society that do not change hands at least once through the market is so small that we can ignore them completely. The fact that every product at some point in its life serves as an object of exchange stamps it as an *exchange-value*: and it is this twofold character of being both a use-value and an exchange-value that makes the product into a commodity.

Let us consider this matter of exchange more closely. What does it mean to say that a car will exchange for a piano? In this instance it means that one use-value is equal to another, qualitatively different, use value. But in what real sense can they be equal? In a material sense they are completely different: they are made out of different materials, they serve different purposes and require completely different types of skill to make. But none the less there must be a sense in which they are the same, otherwise they could not exchange for each other. Logically, it is only possible to compare quantitatively items which are already qualitatively identical. Therefore, items which have a different material form, like a piano and a car, and yet which are equal in exchange, must have something in common and have an equal amount of it. This common property of *all* commodities is human labour.

But, it can be objected, the type of labour that makes a piano is quite different from the type of labour that makes a car. In fact, if we think of labour from the point of view of the actual tasks it performs, that is, if we think in terms of *concrete labour*, it is obviously true that there are many different forms of labour varying according to the nature of the use-values they produce, and that these different forms are not directly comparable with each other. For example, the particular types of labour and skills used in car manufacturing are not those required to make pianos. But just as use-values that are materially different from each other and satisfy quite different needs, share the common property of being use-values, so the different forms of concrete labour share the common property of all being labour. This can be called *abstract labour* and all the different types of concrete labour, the different types that make pianos and cars for instance, are all different forms of abstract labour.

Abstract labour is the quality that all commodities have in common. Its crystallisation in the form of a commodity gives that commodity *value*. In other words value is abstract labour embodied in a commodity.[1]

[1] The common property of all commodities is the 'same unsubstantial reality . . . a mere congelation of homogeneous human labour, of labour-power expended without regard to its mode of expenditure. All that these things now tell us is, that human labour-power has been expended in their production, that human labour is embodied in them. When looked at as crystals of this social substance common to them all, they are – Values' (Marx, *Capital*, vol. 1, p. 5). Value, understood in this way, is definitely *not* price, and when we talk of the value of a commodity we do not mean its

This concept of value might appear abstract and for this reason quite unreal. Orthodox economists have often objected to it on these grounds and prefer to think in terms of price which is certainly more concrete and evident. The confusion is increased by the fact that in common usage abstract and unreal are frequently taken to mean the same thing. But because a process or phenomenon is not immediately apparent to our senses does not mean that it does not exist or that it is unreal. The labour, for instance, that is contained within a car or any other commodity, is not apparent if we examine the car itself. If we broke the car down to its components we would not find any labour: at the same time nobody would argue that a car could exist without human labour. Similarly, abstract labour exists within concrete labour though there is no way of seeing it or proving its existence empirically. But its existence can be demonstrated by theoretical argument. It is an abstraction whose reality is demonstrated every time one commodity exchanges for another and every time workers are paid for their work.[2]

---

price: nor is there any implication that the rate at which commodities will exchange for each other in practice is strictly proportional to their values. On the contrary: 'The possibility . . . of quantitative incongruity between price and magnitude of value, or the deviation of the former from the latter is inherent in the price form itself' (Marx, *Capital*, vol. 1, p. 75). Moreover, it is clear that a commodity has value, is produced, before it is exchanged, so that value is not a phenomenon of exchange at all. What exchange does is to make the value of the individual commodity apparent. '. . . the relation between the values of two commodities supplies us with the simplest expression of the value of a single commodity' (Marx, *Capital*, vol. 1, p. 15). At the same time it is quite consistent to talk of price being *governed* by value in the sense that all exchanges in the economy taken together must conform to the law of value, although individual acts of exchange do not take place at prices strictly equivalent to relative value. In the last analysis this is only another way of saying that supply and demand, the market, are determined by production and consumption and not vice versa. The law of value is the way in which this determination is exercised in the special conditions of capitalist society.

[2] Although abstract labour is an abstraction in the conventional sense of being a creation of the mind, it is not the same as the arbitrary assumptions made by economists when they construct their models. For it already corresponds directly with reality, and, in a sense, already contains a theory of that reality. 'This reduction (of concrete to abstract labour) appears to be an abstraction, but it is an abstraction that is made every day in the social process of production' (Marx, *Critique of Political Economy*, p. 30).

In the process of exchange qualitatively different phenomena, whether different use-values or different forms of concrete labour, are reduced to a single common denominator.
This common denominator is value or crystallised abstract
labour.

Value defined as crystallised abstract labour takes account
of production both as a material process as well as a social
process. It takes account of the material aspect of production
directly since abstract labour can only become crystallised
through the process of material production. Abstract labour
can only enter a commodity, i.e. a commodity can only acquire
its value, as a result of material production. At the same time
abstract labour is a 'social substance', and value which is
crystallised labour therefore immediately invokes the social
aspect of production. The meaning of this will become clearer
as we discuss the law of value but we can illustrate the point
by returning briefly to the process of exchange.

At first sight a capitalist economy appears as a complex mass
of exchanges between inanimate objects with men as mere by-
standers. Thus, people talk of the price of cars, the price of
pianos, and so on, as though commodities were the main actors
on stage. 'But it is plain that commodities cannot go to market
and make exchanges of their own account.'[3] To this extent
every exchange is an exchange between men and the commodity is only the material moment in a social act: i.e. an act
that brings men into relation with each other. But even this
material moment represented by the material form of the commodity, i.e. the car or the piano as the object of the exchange,
is not quite as material as it seems at first sight. For the commodity as an object of value is crystallised abstract labour and
what is taking place in an act of exchange is the exchange of
one mass of crystallised labour for another. Exchange is the
exchange of human labour in a congealed form. 'There is a
definite social relation between men that assumes, in their
eyes, the fantastic form of a relation between things.'[4]

The social nature of commodity production and exchange

[3] Marx, *Capital*, vol. 1, p. 56.
[4] Marx, *Capital*, vol. 1, p. 43. '. . . [men's] own social actions take the form
of an action of objects, which rule producers instead of being ruled by
them' (p. 46).

becomes clear when we disregard the material form of commodities altogether and consider them simply as objects of value. We can then see the capitalist economy as a complex arrangement of value production and exchange. This might appear abstract but it is not unreal. It bears the same relation to the actual events of daily economic life as the equations of force and stress bear to a suspension bridge on any other construction which clearly cannot be analysed through a description of the numerous girders and so on of which it is composed. The law theory of value moves behind reality: it never forsakes it.

2. *The circuit of capital*

In Chapter 2 we defined the concept of surplus as the difference between social production and the level of consumption necessary for this production to take place. In capitalist society this surplus is appropriated by capital and assumes the social form of *profit*.

To explain how this happens we begin with the circuit of capital:

$$M - C_{MP}^{L} \dots P \dots C' - M'$$

where M represents money; C, a commodity; L, labour power; and MP, the means of production, the collective term for the instruments and materials of labour. A business starts its activities with its capital in the form of money, which it uses to hire labour and purchase the necessary means of production $(M - C_{MP}^{L})$. These it then organises in the process of production (P) to produce a new commodity $(C_{MP}^{L} \dots P \dots C')$. The final stage of the circuit $(C' - M')$ sees the sale of this new commodity and the transformation of the capital advanced in its production back into money. But the amount of money (M') at the end of the circuit need not equal the amount at the beginning (M). On the contrary, where a firm makes a profit M' exceeds M by the amount of this profit. On this basis the rate of profit can be calculated as $M' - M/M$.

The prime suffixes $(')$ are attached to C and M in the second part of the circuit $(C'$ and $M')$ to show that while they still represent commodities and money respectively as C and M in the first part, before the process of production takes place, they represent a different *C* and a different *M*. But the nature of the difference varies in the two instances. The difference between *M* and *M'* is purely *quantitative* for the nature of the money is the same at both poles of the circuit. The only possible difference between one sum of money and another is its size: we have just seen that this difference in size makes up the profit of the firm.

But the difference between *C* and *C'* is in the first instance *qualitative*. The new commodity produced by the firm (*C'*) is materially quite different from the commodities it purchases at the beginning of the circuit, the labour-power and the means of production which make its production possible. In the case of any one particular use-value, say for instance cars, *C'* takes the form of cars, while *C* includes various types of concrete labour-power – the labour-power of fitters, welders, line-workers and so on; raw materials such as steel, tin, rubber and plastic; and machinery such as conveyor belts and lathes. Thus, the circuit as a whole consists of two sets of changes: (1) a quantitative change in the value of capital advanced which is evident in the difference between *M'* and *M*; and (2) a qualitative difference in the material nature of the commodities in question which is apparent in the difference between *C* and *C'*. A quantitative difference in the value of capital also exists in *C'*, since the new commodities possess greater value than those that make up the means of production. The transformation *C – C'* is both quantitative and qualitative. However, for the moment let us concentrate solely on the qualitative side of this change.

A moment's reflection shows that it can only be achieved through a process of material production. To convert one set of commodities (*C*) into another wholly different commodity (*C'*) requires the expenditure of labour, and in a modern industrial economy the use of elaborate tools and machinery. But while it is obviously true that the qualitative transformation of *C* into *C'* requires material production, it is less obvious, but no less true, that the quantitative change of *M* into *M'* – i.e. profit – can only find its origin in the same productive activity. Stated more precisely: the sum of profits of all the businesses in a capitalist economy, that is *social profits* or the *profits of social capital,* must originate in the sphere of production, and not in the sphere of circulation or exchange.

In the last chapter we saw that in any given period of time, say one year, a part of the social product must be used to cover the items of necessary consumption. These fall into two categories: (1) the personal consumption of the direct producers, in capitalist society the wage-labourers; and (2) the productive consumption of the means of production. If these are not met in full the social productive forces will be diminished and the scale of production will fall in subsequent years. In capitalist society these general social requirements present themselves to an individual firm as the need to pay wages to its workers, to meet the bills of its various suppliers and to make good the depreciation of its buildings and machinery. The surplus left over after sales constitutes profit. It is clear that if the level of social production is to be maintained, profits must be *residual* by nature. In other words social profit is the difference between what is produced in a capitalist economy and the level of consumption necessary to achieve that production.

Contrast this with the common view that profits are made through buying and selling, through buying cheap and selling dear. It is true that profits are *realised* through selling $(C' - M')$ and that this presupposes a previous act of buying $(M - C_{MP}^L)$. But this does not mean that these acts of exchange form the real source of profit. By analogy, an electric light is turned on (i.e. realised) by the flick of a switch, but this does not generate the electricity that allows the light to burn. The confusion of the realisation of profits with their real production generally arises from the tendency to view the process of capitalist production from the standpoint of the individual firm. This confusion is compounded by the existence of specialised firms which make profits through buying and selling without engaging in production at all – wholesalers, retailers and banks fall into this category: the more cheaply they buy and the more expensively they sell the greater their profit. But this obvious fact has no bearing one way or another on the general proposition that profits as a whole originate in the sphere of production as the surplus of the social product over the consumption necessary for its production. The magnitude of social profit cannot be affected by acts of exchange: on the other hand, its distribution between different firms is subject to market transactions. It is through buying and selling that firms compete for their share of total profits. But the forces that determine the distribution of profits must not be mistaken for those that determine its magnitude. They are of strictly secondary importance. For example, it makes no difference to the length of a piece of rope, that is say twelve feet, whether it be divided into two pieces of six feet, six pieces of two feet or so on; even if those competing over its division make the most strenuous efforts to increase their share and on occasions go as far as employing whole armies to destroy each other.[5]

'3. *The magnitude of value*

All commodities require labour to produce and therefore all commodities possess value. But different commodities possess different amounts of value depending upon the amount of labour their production requires. Thus, a pencil which requires less labour to produce than a car possesses less value than a car. In general, the value of commodities varies directly with amount of labour *socially necessary* for their production.[6]

[5] 'In practical commerce, capitalist A can screw capitalist B. The one pockets what the other loses. If we add them both together, then the sum of their exchange=the sum of the labour time objectified within it, of which capitalist A has merely pocketed more than his share in relation to capitalist B. From all the profits made by capital, i.e. the total mass of capitalists, there is to be deducted (1) the constant part of capital; (2) the wage, or, the amount of objectified labour time necessary in order to produce living labour capacity. They can therefore divide nothing among themselves other than the surplus value. The proportion – just or unjust – in which they distribute this surplus value among themselves alters absolutely nothing about exchange or about the exchange relations between capital and labour' (Marx, *Grundrisse*, p. 424).

[6] Although value has a quantitative aspect this cannot be measured in practice. There is no way we can measure the value of a pencil, or a car, or any commodity directly. Nor can value be measured indirectly through relative prices. Attempts to do so, or to criticise the law of value on the grounds that it cannot be done, miss the point altogether. Despite outward appearances the law of value is not a theory of relative prices: its object of concern is the relationship between capital and labour. Throughout *Capital*, Marx uses exchange relationships to illustrate his theory, but in many cases there are only illustrations not to be taken literally. The first chapter of volume 1 contains a complex argument which shows that the exchange of commodities is not of central importance and that the real nature and

This qualification, that it is the amount of socially necessary labour, and not simply the amount of labour in each individual case, that determines the value of commodities, is extremely important. Firstly, it precludes anomalies that the products of inefficient workers possess more value than the similar products of efficient workers on the grounds that they have taken longer to produce. At each level of technology there is a certain average amount of labour required for the production of every commodity. This is the amount of labour that can be said to be socially necessary, and this is the amount of labour that determines values.[7] Secondly, the value of commodities does not remain constant. As the productivity of labour changes through time, owing to developments such as an advance in technical knowledge, the amount of labour required to produce a commodity falls and the value of the commodity falls with it. Thus, as productivity rises less labour time is required to produce any given amount of commodities. Or to look at the same

---

significance of exchange cannot be understood in its own terms. Marx's theory, i.e. that commodities can only exchange because they are first objects of value and that the nature of value production is therefore the first thing to be considered, has been widely misunderstood by the economists who, confined within the narrow restrictions they have imposed upon themselves, are unable to give importance to any other question than these that concern relative prices. In other words, they take their own definition of economics so much for granted that they are unable to see that Marx has an alternative approach and that the way in which this alternative is constituted is a definitive criticism of their own. Moreover, Marx's scientific method is quite different from that of orthodox economics, which telescopes its theoretical and analytical concepts into one. Thus they will not use a concept in theory which is not immediately applicable in practice. Joan Robinson has called this 'hard-headedness' in contradistinction to which Marx's concept of value is 'metaphysical'. See Joan Robinson, *Economic Philosophy* (London: Penguin, 1962), chapters 1 and 2. But the fact that we cannot measure value directly is no evidence that it does not exist, nor that it is not quantitative. Value is the reality inside reality. We cannot measure gravity directly, or isolate it in practice from the phenomena that it holds in relation, but this does not mean that it is metaphysical nor that its effects cannot be perceived quantitatively.

[7] 'The labour time socially necessary is that required to produce an article under the normal conditions of production, and with the average degree of skill and intensity prevalent at the time . . . that which determines the magnitude of the value of any article is the amount of labour socially necessary . . . for its production' (Marx, *Capital*, vol. 1, p. 6).

development in another way, as productivity rises a given value of production is expressed by a larger mass of commodities.[8]

The value of commodities is determined by the amount of labour socially necessary for their production. This labour enters the commodity in two ways: directly through living labour, and indirectly through the means of production. A simple example will illustrate this point.

Let us imagine a car factory with an annual output of 10,000 cars which require, all told, 6 mn man hours to produce and which therefore have a value measured by 6 mn man hours. Assume half this value is produced directly by living labour in the factory, which will be the case if 1500 workers are employed for 40 hours a week, 50 weeks a year. In this case the other half will be produced indirectly and enter the cars through the means of production. Consequently, the means of production – the machines and the materials – upon which the living labour in the car plant works, must already contain 3 mn hours of labour before they enter the factory. In other words, 3 mn man hours of labour have been taken up producing the machines and the materials before the production of cars proper begins. This indirect labour is as indispensable to production as direct labour and it cannot be left out of account.

To be clear about the exact nature of the contribution of the means of production to the value of the output, it must be remembered that commodities possess value in so far as they are the products of human labour. In other words, only human labour can produce value. Thus, the way in which value is defined precludes the possibility of machines or other means of production adding any *new* value to the commodities in which they become embodied in the process of production. On the other hand the means of production do contribute to the value of the product in so far as they yield up the value they already possess when they enter the factory.

Assume that the part of the means of production in our car

---

[8] 'An increase in the quantity of use-values is an increase in material wealth. With two coats two men can be clothed, with one coat only one man. Nevertheless, an increased quantity of material wealth may correspond to a simultaneous fall in the magnitude of its value' (Marx, *Capital*, vol. 1, p. 13).

factory which consists of instruments of labour – that is the conveyor belts, the lathes and so on – requires 2 mn man hours to produce, and therefore possesses value to the extent of 2 mn man hours. As these instruments are used by the workers in the process of production, i.e. as they are productively consumed, this value is used up. But it is not destroyed: what happens is that it passes from the machines and enters into the cars so that at the end of the year the machines no longer possess any value and are completely depreciated. But the cars which have been produced with them will contain all their value. Exactly the same happens with regard to the materials of labour, the tin, steel, rubber and plastic out of which the workers produce the cars. Originally these materials must have been natural objects and in that form did not possess any value. But to become materials of labour in a car plant all these natural materials must be processed by labour and as a result become commodities and receptacles of value. In our example, 1 mn man hours of labour is required to transform them from natural objects into suitable materials for car workers: 1 mn man hours of labour expended in steel mills, chemical plants and so on. As the materials are productively consumed in the car factory this value, and no more, is transferred to the cars. Thus, as living labour works in a factory it not only adds value to its product directly, but by productively consuming means of production it adds their value indirectly to the final product. Thus, without denying the material indispensability of means of production, we can none the less assert that labour is the only source of value.

The passive role of the means of production, particularly of the instruments of labour, in the process of value production; their ability to impart only that value which they already possess and no more, and the fact that they are nothing other than products of labour themselves, is less apparent in a modern industrial economy than in one where the organisation of production is more rudimentary and technology is less advanced. If for the moment we consider the process of production in a simple one-man economy, we can highlight the specific features of modern capitalist production that obscure this point.

Assume an isolated individual faced with the task of digging himself a shelter in the side of a hill. While it would presumably be possible for him to do this with bare hands, let us assume he fashions himself a spade of some sort from whatever natural materials lay about. Without getting involved in inconsequential details of this analogy, we can see that if our individual spends 4 hours making himself a simple spade which is just adequate for his task, and a further 4 hours using it, he will in total have spent 8 hours digging his shelter. The value of this shelter will be measured by this 8 hours of labour, 4 of which were applied indirectly in making the spade and 4 of which were applied directly. The value produced in the first 4 hours will at the end of that time be embodied in the spade.[9] During the second 4 hours, while the actual digging is taking place, the spade is productively consumed and the value it contains is transferred to the shelter. In other words, while the spade becomes materially indispensable to the process of digging, it can add no more value than it already possesses. Looking at the process of production as a whole, we see that it has involved a division of labour: half the labour time has been spent on the task of making the tool, the other half on using it. But because we have assumed only one worker, this division of labour appears as the division of a single worker's time. We can therefore be under no illusions about what has taken place. Eight hours of labour has been spent on the product. The fact that different types of concrete labour have been used – spade-making and digging – does not change this one iota. The spade is unambiguously the product of labour: in this case it is the product of the same worker who uses it. It has no real existence outside the worker: it was he who made it and it cannot act as a spade unless he uses it as such. As a product of labour it contains a definite amount of value which can be transferred to the final product; but it cannot transfer more value than it already possesses.[10] It has no intrinsic magical properties.

[9] We are tacitly assuming here that the instruments of labour – machines and so on – actually wear out in a single year, whereas in practice they last several years. This assumption does not alter the fundamentals of value production in any way and it is used here purely for the sake of simplicity. See Chapter 6 below.

[10] We are of course assuming that the spade is completely worn out and useless when the shelter is finished. If this is not the case the matter is not affected in any fundamental way, except the form in which value exists. Suppose that the spade does not wear out completely, but is only one

But three aspects of contemporary industrial capitalist production obscure the real nature of the part played by instruments of labour in the process of production, lending a certain plausibility to the erroneous impression that these instruments play an independent role and contribute to new value.

Firstly, there is the division of labour, without which the production and use of instruments of production is impossible. With modern industrial production this division of labour is highly advanced, and almost invariably the workers who make machines are different from those who use them. Moreover, labour is further divided through time and the more complex the technology the further apart in time will be the production of machines and their use. This separation of the two sets of workers, those who make machines and those who use them, makes the machines appear independent of labour altogether. Certainly, this is the way they appear in the factories where they are used.

Secondly, most modern machines, unlike tools, are not immediately dependent upon the worker for their power; nor does the precision with which they can operate depend upon the skill of the worker who uses them. When he works with a tool, the worker remains to a large extent in control of his labour, but with a machine he largely loses this control. In fact, the situation has often been entirely reversed, and the pace and nature of labour becomes wholly determined by the machine, which appears to be less the product of labour than its master. But the exercise of this domination requires the existence of certain 'social' relationships between the worker and the machine and these constitute the third aspect of modern industrial production which we must note here. In the capitalist factory the worker does not own the machine on which he works; in fact, he has no legal rights over it whatsoever. In a

---

one quarter depreciated and our lone worker could use it to dig three more shelters if he wished. In this case only one quarter of its value is productively consumed in digging; the other three quarters remaining intact. On this assumption the value of the shelter will be equivalent to 5 hours of labour, 4 hours of living labour plus 1 hour transferred from the spade. The remaining value created by the worker, equivalent to 3 hours of labour, remain in the spade, so the total value of production is still equivalent to 8 hours; only this labour is now embodied in two products.

legal and in a real social sense, the machine is independent of the worker.

But these complexities of capitalist production only obscure the nature of the instruments of labour, they do not change it. No matter how far the division of labour has developed, how advanced and automated the machines, and irrespective of the system of property relations within which they are used, all instruments of labour must originally be the products of labour. As such, the only value they possess, and can bestow, is that which labour has previously embodied in them. Moreover, they cannot even bestow this value unless living labour makes use of them. From the point of view of value production machinery, for all its material complexity, remains only the passive reflex of labour.

4. *Profit*

In the circuit of capital, $M - C^L_{MP} \ldots P \ldots C' - M'$, the difference between M' and M, the value with which the capitalist finishes minus that with which he starts, is the magnitude of profit. Two possible sources for this profit have now been excluded: first, buying and selling; second, the means of production. The only one that remains is labour itself.

While it is possible for an individual capitalist to increase his profit through buying and selling, capital as a whole is unable to do this. As our concern is with social capital we must firmly exclude exchange as a source of profit. This is not difficult. When we examine an economy as a whole, we see that each year it turns out a social product with a definite amount of value. This product, when it takes the form of commodities, changes hands through the market. But these acts of buying and selling cannot affect its value; and the sum of the total exchanges each year must therefore add up exactly to it. In other words, if the social product takes 10 mn man hours to produce, and the sum of all transactions in money terms adds up to £20 mn; 10 mn man hours equals £20 mn, and 1 man hour equals £2. If we now think of individual commodities as *representative* parts of the social product, as the sum of their market prices must add up to an amount equivalent to their total value, it follows that each one of them will exchange at price equivalent to its value. Thus, if a car and piano, as representative commodities, require the same amount of labour to produce, they will exchange on the market at the same price. A more elaborate car which requires twice as much labour will exchange at double this price. Clearly exchange relations regulated in this way cannot be a source of profit since the buying and selling prices of commodities must be the same – i.e. their value. Thus, equivalent exchange imposes on the individual capital those conditions which apply to capital as a whole.

The argument lying behind equivalent exchange has been widely ignored or misunderstood with the result that the law of value has been mistakenly interpreted as a labour theory of price, whose aim is to explain the price of individual commodities in terms of the amount of labour their production requires. But in the law of value the prices of individual commodities are of strictly secondary importance; its main concern is the relationship between social capital on the one side and the class of workers as a whole on the other. In so far as it features the activities of individual capitalists and particular groups of workers, it does so purely by way of illustration, for these individual capitalists and groups of workers are not important in their own right but only as representatives of capital and labour respectively. They are the average capitalist and the average worker. Similarly, when we discuss particular commodities like cars, it is not the car as a car that is of importance, but the car as a part of the social product. Thus, if it is impossible for the whole class of capitalists to make profits through acts of exchange we assume that the individual representative average capitalist is unable to do so either. But it should not be thought that the activities of individual capitalists and particular groups of workers and the production of individual commodities are considered unimportant in their own right. On the contrary, according to the law of value, the process of production in the individual capitalist enterprise has great significance, but this cannot be grasped without the nature of capitalist enterprise in general having been first understood. And it is with this general nature of capitalist production, with the relationship between social capital and social labour, and not with the price of individual commodities, that the law of value is concerned in the first instance. The assumption of the equivalence of exchange is nothing more than a way of abstracting from specific features of individual firms in order to bring the general nature of capitalism into focus.

Having said this, we can look at circuit of capital of an individual firm, knowing that what we are looking at is not any particular firm but an average firm, representative of social capital. As such, it is unable to derive any profits from either of the acts of exchange in which it necessarily engages. It cannot buy the materials it needs for production below their value, nor can it sell its product above its value. Furthermore, its means of production cannot yield value they do not already possess. But since it is forced to buy them at value, what they contribute to the value of the final product is exactly equal to what was paid for them. Thus, they make no net addition to value, and therefore cannot be a source of profit. As this is true of all the *impersonal* agencies in the sphere of production, labour alone, the *personal* agency, must be the source of profit.

Labour enters the circuit of capital in its first phase, $M - C^L$. In this act of exchange the worker is the seller and the capitalist the buyer. The commodity that changes hands is the worker's capacity to labour, or his *labour-power*, for a definite period of time – an hour, a week, a month. Just as when a person who hires a car is in fact buying the use of that car for the duration of the hiring time, so the capitalist who hires a worker buys his labour-power for a particular period. The contractual nature of the relationship between the capitalist and the worker plus the fact that a worker cannot sell his labour-power unless he is personally present, tend to obscure the simple exchange relation which lies at its root. The capitalist is a buyer; the worker is a seller, and the object of their transaction is labour-power. In three important respects labour-power is a commodity like any other.

Firstly, labour-power is an exchange value in the sense that it is not used or consumed by the worker who possesses it for his own purposes, but is sold to another. It is paid for as any other commodity: the value it commands in exchange on the market is the *wage*. The existence of labour-power as a commodity is thus implicit in the idea of wage-labour.

Secondly, labour-power is a use value. It fashions its materials into products which satisfy some social use. Except where the worker performs some service directly, as is the case with, say, a hairdresser, labour-power derives its quality of being a use value, from the fact that it produces tangible commodities that are use values. But while its quality of being a use-value derives from the commodity it produces, its magnitude as a use-value depends upon its own size measured in time. In the case of the car factory, 1500 workers are employed for 40 hours a week, 50 weeks a year. The labour-power they sell is a use-value because the cars they produce are use-values. Collectively, the workers sell 3 mn hours of labour-power: individually, each worker sells 2000 hours. These figures measure the magnitude of the use-value of the commodity, labour-power, which the capitalist buys from its workers.

Thirdly labour-power possesses value. It requires labour to produce and like any other commodity its value is equal to the amount of this labour that is socially necessary for its production. This is not immediately evident because labour-power is not produced directly in the same way as other commodities – there is not a labour process whose immediate product is labour-power. Labour-power does not have a separate tangible material existence like most commodities; it cannot be separated from the living worker before it is consumed. 'By labour-power', Marx wrote, 'is to be understood the aggregate of the mental and physical capabilities in a human being which he exercises whenever he produces a use-value of any description.'[11] Thus the production of labour-power is in the first instance the production of the living human being and while this involves complex social institutions, it also requires material products such as food, clothing and shelter. In capitalist society these take the form of commodities and have a definite amount of value – this is the value of labour-power.[12]

[11] Marx, *Capital*, vol. 1, p. 145.

[12] The value of labour-power is equal to the value of the commodities that comprise necessary consumption. With reference to the individual worker, Marx writes: 'His means of subsistence must . . . be sufficient to maintain him in his normal state as a labouring individual. His natural wants, such as food, clothing, fuel and housing, vary according to the climate and other conditions of his country. On the other hand, the number and extent of his so-called necessary wants, as also the means of satisfying them, are themselves the product of historical development, and depend

In our example of car production the 1500 workers sell to the capitalist 3 mn hours of labour-power each year. But in order to do this they must consume a mass of commodities which, let us suppose, take 1·5 mn hours to produce. In other words they sell a commodity whose use-value is 3 mn hours of labour, but whose *value* is equivalent to only half that amount, 1·5 mn hours. The wage relation is an exchange like any other in so far as it is governed not by the use-value of the commodity, but by its value.[13] Thus although the workers sell a use-value which is capable of producing a value equivalent to 3 mn hours, the value of this commodity is only 1·5 mn hours, and this is the value they received from capitalist – i.e. the value of the wage. In other words, the worker is paid a value wage equal to the value of his labour-power, *not* to the value his

---

therefore to a great extent on the degree of civilisation of a country, more particularly on the conditions under which, and consequently on the habits and degree of comfort in which, the class of free-labourers has been formed' (Marx, *Capital*, vol. 1, pp. 149–50). Necessary consumption is thus not a simple biological minimum, although it must always cover this minimum. In advanced capitalist societies the social dimension of necessity is largely determined by capital itself and necessary consumption consists not only of commodities that satisfy the needs of the working class, but of commodities that it is necessary for capital to sell to the working class. Thus so-called luxury items such as cars and television become items of necessary consumption in a phase of capitalist development when so much production is organised for the consumer market.

In this context it is interesting to note a discrepancy in the way that national income is accounted. Allowance is always made for the wear and tear of capital and depreciation is always deducted from gross income. But wages are treated as though they were *all* net income and no allowance is made for the wear and tear of the worker. In the structure of personal taxation a concession to reality is made by force of circumstances and workers are granted personal allowances for themselves and their families.

[13] In practice there is no more reason for expecting labour-power to exchange at a price equivalent to its value than any other commodity. Only if the wage falls below value for any length of time working class consumption will fall below its necessary level and the capacity of the class to produce, and reproduce itself, will be impaired. On the other hand, if the wage rises far above the value of labour-power and approaches the new value produced by labour, surplus value must fall, and capital will lose the inducement to set new production in motion. Thus from one side and the other, there are powerful forces in play that tend to keep wages in close contact with the value of labour-power.

labour-power produces. The difference between these two values is the real and only source of profit.

Assuming that one hour of labour can be expressed in money terms as, say, £1, we can illustrate this argument in more conventional terms that are perhaps easier to understand. In these terms the source of profit of the car manufacturer whom we have assumed to be a representative capitalist can be shown as follows:

	£mn
Value derived from the means of production	3·0
Value added by living labour	3·0
Gross value of 10,000 cars	6·0
less:	
Cost of means of production	3·0
Wages	1·5
	1·5

The way in which this £1·5 mn is acquired meets every condition set down. None of it comes through buying cheap and selling dear since every commodity exchanges at its value. The final output, the cars, sells at its value, and the capitalist purchases at their values all the commodities he needs to undertake production. At the same time no profit is derived from the means of production: they add £3.0 mn to the value of the cars on the one hand, but cost the capitalist £3.0 mn on the other. The profit is the difference between the value created by labour, and the value of the necessary commodities consumed by the workers. As we have seen, this latter represents the value of the labour-power that the workers sell and the value the capitalist pays them in wages. In short, the capitalist pays the workers the full value of their labour-power: he makes his profits without resort to sharp dealing and cheating.

5. *Surplus value*

The difference in value between what living labour produces and the necessary consumption of the workers is *surplus value*. In absolute terms surplus value equals profit. But in relative terms they are quite different. They have a quite different

significance which their equality of absolute size tends to con-
ceal.

To understand the difference between surplus value and
profit, let us return to the circuit of capital, $M - C^L_{MP} \dots P \dots$
$C' - M'$. We have seen

$$\text{profit} = M' - M \qquad (1)$$

$$\text{and the rate of profit} = \frac{M' - M}{M} \qquad (2)$$

On the assumption that all commodities exchange at their value

$$M = MP + L \qquad (3)$$

This can be expressed as

$$M = c + v \qquad (4)$$

where c represents constant capital; and v, variable capital.
The logic behind the choice of these terms is as follows: The
total capital advanced at the start of the circuit of capital can
be divided into two categories: (1) the part advanced on the
means of production whose value remains constant throughout
the circuit of capital – hence constant capital; and (2) the part
advanced to employ labour whose value varies throughout the
circuit – hence variable capital.

$$M' - M = s \qquad (5)$$

where s represents surplus value;

and $$M' = c + v + s \qquad (6)$$

This means that the value of output is equal to the value of the
constant and variable capital consumed in its production plus
surplus value.

Expressed in these terms the *rate of profit*, $\dfrac{M' - M}{M}$ becomes
$\dfrac{s}{c+v}$. On the other hand the *rate of surplus value*, the ratio of the
surplus produced by labour to the value it receives is $\dfrac{s}{v}$. Thus,
while profit and surplus value are equal in an absolute
sense, they are different in a relative sense: the rate of
profit clearly does not equal the rate of surplus value. Since
it relates surplus value to the total capital advanced, to both

constant and variable capital, the rate of profit is always less than the rate of surplus value, which relates surplus value only to variable capital. This simple difference carries enormous implications.

To start with the rate of profit. This is the ratio of the greatest concern to capital and a moment's consideration shows why. The rate of profit not only measures the rate of return on the total capital advanced, but also, and more importantly, the rate at which a business can expand. The example of the car firm illustrates this clearly. The profit of the firm at the end of the year amounts to £1·5 mn and this would allow the firm to employ another 1500 workers and thereby double its labour force. But if it did this it would have no funds left to buy means of production to set these additional employees to work. All it can do is to employ an additional 500 workers which requires £0·5 mn and use the remaining £1·0 mn to buy the necessary means of production. In other words, it can expand its activities by one third, that is by an amount equal to its rate of profit. But while the rate of profit has this practical significance for the businessman, it is a very misleading indicator for the economist, since by relating surplus value to both constant and variable capital it gives the impression that both parts of capital, that is machinery as well as labour, are the source of surplus. The rate of profit obscures what the rate of surplus value makes clear, namely, that profit is unpaid labour.[14]

The rate of surplus value in the case of the car firm is 100 per cent. This indicates that the workers receive only one half of the total value they produce; the other half is taken by the business as profit. The rate of surplus value is thus the ratio of paid to unpaid labour; it is the *rate of exploitation*. It provides the clearest possible indication of the relationship between capital and labour, and since this relationship is the central preoccupation of the law of value, its importance is central.

Finally, we can note how the concept of surplus value engages with the law of social reproduction in capitalist society. In Chapter 2 we defined surplus in general, that is, for all modes of production, as the difference between material pro-

[14] 'Profit . . . is the same as surplus value, only in a mystified form that is nonetheless a necessary out growth of the capitalist mode of production' (Marx, *Capital* vol. 3 (London: Lawrence and Wishart, 1971), p. 36).

duction and the consumption necessary to achieve it. This necessary consumption comprises the means of production used up in the process of production, which require replacement, and the personal consumption of the direct producers. In capitalist society these general social requirements present themselves to the individual capitalist as the need to maintain or replace his equipment, and the obligation to pay his raw material suppliers for the materials he uses, and pay wages to his employees. On the assumption that the prices he has to pay are equivalent to the value of the commodities he purchases, the *cost of production*, i.e. constant plus variable capital, will equal the value of necessary consumption. As we have been considering a representative average capitalist, it follows that the cost price of production of social capital will equal the level of socially necessary consumption, or the level of consumption necessary to achieve basic social reproduction. Where a surplus is produced in capitalist society, it will show up as an excess of production over the cost price of production. In short, surplus in capitalist society is the difference between the value of production and the value of the constant and variable capital advanced to bring it about, i.e. surplus value. Thus, the law of social reproduction works in the special conditions of capitalist society in this way: the circuit of production and consumption operates through the circuit of capital: socially necessary consumption assumes the form of constant and variable capital in this circuit: surplus becomes surplus value and accrues to capital in the form of profit.

6. *Wages and circuit of labour*

We must now examine capitalist production from the other side and consider the circuit of labour and the nature of wages.

When we first consider wages it seems that the most significant questions to ask concern their size. How much is the money wage? What will it buy? What is the real wage? But although they are important these questions should not be posed first. Although the level of wages has immediate and direct effects upon the living standards of the working class and is one of the primary magnitudes of the economy, it is of secondary importance in understanding the general nature of wages. In itself, it sheds no light on the social relations of production which the wage presupposes and expresses. By analogy: if our concern was with 'the ladder', the length of any particular ladder, or even variations in the length of ladders among different countries and in different periods, would tell us nothing itself about the nature of ladders, what they can be used for, and so on. Excessive concentration on the level of wages diverts attention from their nature. So long as they are considered in quantitative terms as £20 a week or £30 a week and so on, the meaning of the wage will remain hidden. To analyse what it is that every wage has in common, it is necessary to disregard size altogether, and consider the wage where its size is zero. Little imagination is required to make this abstraction for it happens in reality every time a worker is unemployed.

Leaving aside unemployment benefit paid by the state,[15] how can a worker maintain himself when he loses his job and cannot find another immediately? Only one possibility is open to him – selling his property and living off the proceeds. But this is not an effective solution.

Firstly, most workers own very little and would have to lower their living standards quite drastically to keep going for any length of time this way. Secondly, working class property is made up almost exclusively of means of consumption which are not substantial enough to act as capital. In the first instance the difference between property and capital is quantitative, but this is a clear instance of where a difference in quantity rapidly becomes one of quality. Few workers own enough to be able to live off their investments without touching the original sums. Assuming an income of £20 a week to be a rough minimum, and the interest rate after tax to be 8 per cent, a person would need around £12,500. Few workers can lay their hands on this sort of money: or to put it another way, not many people with this type of free cash work in jobs where long-term unemployment is a real threat. If an unemployed worker could realise as much as, say, half this amount he would

15 The case for ignoring social security benefits in this context is that if they were sufficiently high to maintain their recipient at a socially acceptable standard and could be drawn as of right without any stigma, the compulsion to work would be removed. Thus in practice they are only paid to a small minority that are unemployed and then on condition that their recipient takes a suitable job if one becomes available.

be forced to 'dig into capital' in order to make ends meet and would sooner or later run out of funds. Thirdly, selling items of consumption often does not pay. Most household goods depreciate rapidly in price, and as many are bought on hire purchase with an interest component that puts the actual buying price above the market price, often they can only be sold at a loss. In many cases selling would only lead to an immediate debt and is therefore not worth while. Anyone who discovers this also learns the secret of private property: it appears that the man owns the property, but in reality the property owns the man. Fourthly, property is often a liability, particularly where it is elaborate: cars have to be taxed and insured; fridges and televisions require electricity and so on. Finally, selling means of consumption as a means of maintaining one's standard of living is, by definition, self-defeating.

For all the reasons the worker, even the high-wage affluent worker, is in the last analysis a proletarian with no property. For what he possesses gives him no independence in the sense that he cannot live off it indefinitely. The only thing he owns which he can sell continuously is his capacity for work, his labour-power. In other words he is compelled to go out to work in order to live. When he has a job, especially one that is interesting and highly paid, this economic necessity fades into the background. The social nature of wage-labour is obscured by the size of the wage. Unemployment, however, by cutting the wage to zero reveals its real nature with brutal clarity.

We can look at the matter in more general terms. Labour-power, we know, is a commodity and as such it possesses use-value. But this can only be realised when it is combined with means of production that allow the worker to produce commodities. Thus to society as a whole, and to capital, the use-value of labour-power is represented by the use-values it creates. But for the working class it has no such direct expression. As workers in general have no independent access to the means of production or even to the product of their labour, for them the use-value of labour-power is the exchange value that can be got in return for it, i.e. the money wage. This allows capital to make the hypocritical claim that the only thing that interests workers is money. The circuit of labour, $L \ldots P - m - c$, where L represents labour, P, production, m, the money wage, and c, the real wage, shows just how false this claim is. Unlike the circuit of capital, $M - C_{MP}^{L} \ldots P \ldots C' - M'$, which is primarily quantitative with monetary gain as its sole purpose, the circuit of labour begins and ends with commodities in the use-value form, showing that is primarily qualitative. The money wage, from being the end of the circuit, is merely a moment to be passed by the worker in his struggle for means of consumption. Moreover it is a moment that capital inserts by separating the working class from its means of production and in this way from its means of consumption.

The existence of the wage as a social category, irrespective of its size, thus at once reaffirms and expresses the structure of society in which labour-power is reduced to a commodity itself. The highly paid workers in the developed countries sell their labour-power for the same reasons as lowly paid workers in the underdeveloped world. As regards their social situation in the process of production both sets of workers are identical. The only difference between them is the rate at which they are exploited, and, paradoxically, it is the highly paid workers who are worse off in this respect.

7. *Real wages and the value of wages*

The apparently simple issue of the level of wages is complicated by the fact that the wage has two dimensions and therefore two magnitudes which do not necessarily change in direct proportion to each other when the wage itself changes.

Consider the final element, c, in the circuit of labour, $L \ldots P \ldots m - c$, which represents the means of consumption the workers purchase with their money wages. As these consist of commodities they have two aspects. On the one hand they are use values – food, clothing and so on; on the other, they are values – congelations of abstract human labour. Both these have their quantitative side, and it is from these that the two magnitudes of the wage arise. Firstly, there is the *real wage*, i.e. the actual number of commodities a worker can buy: a *mass of use values*. Secondly, there is the *value of the wage*, which is determined by the amount of labour time socially necessary for the production of this mass. For example, suppose that workers consume only one commodity – flour. The real wage equals the amount of flour they can buy, while the value of the wage is equal to the value of this flour – i.e. the amount of labour its production requires.

Now consider a situation where the real wage increases by 100 per cent and workers are able to buy twice as many use-values as they could previously. What happens to the value of wages? Clearly it will also rise by 100 per cent if the value of wage-goods remains constant; but if this value should change, then the value of the wage must change by a different amount. Assuming for the sake of simplicity only one wage-good, flour, a doubling of the real wage can mean 2 mn tons purchased as opposed to 1 mn. If, in the first instance, 10 hours of labour are required to produce a single ton of flour, the initial value of the wage is equivalent to 10 mn labour hours. As the real wage doubles the value of wages can change in four possible ways:

(1) If the value of flour remains constant, the value of the wage doubles (to 20 mn hours) – i.e. it increases at the same rate as the real wage.
(2) If the value of flour rises (to 20 hours a ton) the value of the wage rises faster (twice as fast) than real wages.
(3) If the value of flour falls (to 5 hours a ton) the value of the wage remains the same while real wages double.
(4) If the value of flour falls proportionately more than real wages rise, the value of the wage will actually fall despite the rise in real wages.

The general formula is as follows:

$$\frac{\Delta w + w}{w} = \frac{\Delta l + l}{l} \quad \frac{\Delta r + r}{r}$$

where w represents the value of the wage; r, the real wage; and l, the value of wage goods.

If
$$\frac{\Delta l + l}{l} = \frac{1}{p}$$

where p represents the *productivity of labour*, then

$$\frac{\Delta w + w}{w} = \frac{1}{p} \quad \frac{\Delta r + r}{r}$$

Consider the definition of the productivity of labour. Clearly the pivotal variable here is Δl for the greater (or smaller) it is, the greater (or smaller) is the rise in productivity. If Δl is positive more labour is required to produce a commodity and we can say that productivity has gone down; if, on the other hand Δl is negative less labour is required in production and we can say that productivity has risen. Thus by changes in the productivity of labour is meant changes in the amount of labour time socially necessary in production. From this it follows that the value of the wage will always rise less rapidly than the real wage if productivity rises: should productivity rise more rapidly than real wages the value of the wage will actually fall.[16]

In the first instance the value of the wage is not immediately significant to the worker who is primarily concerned with what he can get for his money – his real wages. With capital, the reverse is true. The value of what it pays for labour-power affects its rate of surplus value and profit much more immediately than what this value represents in the size of the mass of commodities that embodies this value.

Assume a situation where the value of a day's labour-power

---

[16] It is the productivity of labour in the wage-good sector alone that directly determines the value of the wage, but here and throughout we assume productivity to be the same in all sectors of the economy, so we can say that the value of wage varies with productivity. However, one possible consequence of different rates of change in productivity between the wage-good sector and the sector which produces constant capital must be noted. Suppose productivity remains constant in the wage-good sector but rises elsewhere, so that the value of the wage and the rate of exploitation stay the same, but the value of means of production fall. Assume a fall of 20 per cent so that a machine previously with a value of £100 now has a value of only £80.

Assume in the initial situation:

$$100c + 100v + 100s = 300o$$
so that: the rate of surplus value $= 100\%$
and the rate of profit $\quad = 50\%$

After the rise in productivity

$$80c + 100v + 100s = 280o$$
so that: the rate of surplus value $= 100\%$
and the rate of profit $\quad = 55.5\%$

The rise in the productivity of labour has brought about an increase in the rate of profit despite the fact that the rate of surplus value has remained the same. Moreover, the share of labour in the total product (v/o) has *risen* from 33% to 35.5%. Thus a rise in labour's share of national income is consistent with a rise in the rate of profit.

is equivalent to a mass of commodities which in index number terms we can set at 100. If a worker can produce a value equivalent to this in half a day, say 4 hours, then daily output will equal 200. Assuming that the value of the wage is equal to the value of labour-power then one half a day's output will go to labour and the other half to capital. In other words, the rate of surplus value or exploitation will be equal to 100 per cent. Now suppose productivity doubles so that daily output rises to 400. It now only takes a worker 2 hours to produce a value equivalent to his former wage, so that he can give his employer 6 hours unpaid work. If real wages remain the same, the rate of surplus value increases to 300 per cent. In so far as the worker is concerned with his real wage (use-value) his situation has not deteriorated; but the capitalist whose object of interest is value is certainly much better off. In other words, the distinction between the two magnitudes of the wage, which appears at first sight to be purely formal, here reveals itself as a real distinction corresponding to the different interests of the two main classes of capitalist society.

Consider another possibility. Suppose the workers are able to force up real wages to, say, 150 as their productivity doubles. They are now much better off in real terms. But so is capital. In absolute terms surplus value rises to 250 and the rate o surplus value goes up to 166 per cent. In other words, although the workers are better off they are exploited at a higher rate.[17]

A rise in real wages, therefore, does not necessarily mean a fall in the rate of exploitation. On the contrary, highly paid workers will almost invariably be the most exploited. Some of the reasons for this are fairly obvious. A lowly paid worker barely able to make ends meet, illiterate, poorly housed, unhealthy, and poorly equipped is much less productive than a highly paid worker who is educated, well-fed and well-equipped. It takes him much longer to produce the equivalent of his wage

[17] It is in terms of a rising rate of exploitation not a falling real wage that the so-called 'doctrine of increasing misery' attributed to Marx must be understood. As the whole of volume 1 of *Capital* is conducted in value terms, no other interpretation is consistent with the general framework of the analysis. For Marx the misery of the working class related to the conditions and rate of its exploitation, not its level of consumption '. . . in proportion as capital accumulates, the lot of the labourers, be his payment high or low, must grow worse' (Marx, *Capital*, vol. 1, p. 661).

and therefore the proportion of the working day he is able to give away free is much lower. The more productive highly paid worker, on the other hand produces his wage in a much shorter time and is therefore able to perform much more surplus labour. By implication, therefore, the affluent workers of the developed countries are much more exploited than the badly paid workers of the underdeveloped world.[18] In fact, given the concept of exploitation that arises from the law of value, no other conclusion seems tenable. How else can one explain the continuous efforts of capital to revolutionise production, except that in doing so, it is able to reduce the value of all commodities in general, and the value of labour-power in particular, and in this way increase its rate of surplus value?

Aside from the obvious problem, dealt with later, of why capital has not pursued this course in the underdeveloped countries where it has relied until recently upon the exploitation of low wage-labour, the law of value poses the most immediate problem for radical development theory. What meaning can be given to its claim that exploitation is the cause of underdevelopment if the rate of exploitation is higher in the developed than in the underdeveloped countries? Or to put the same question in a different way: capitalism has undeniably brought about development in one part of the world, why did it not do

[18] There is every indication that Marx took a higher rate of exploitation in the developed countries for granted. For instance, when comparing a European (i.e. a developed) country with an Asian (i.e. underdeveloped) one he assumed the rate of surplus value to be higher in the former as a matter of course – 100 per cent compared with only 20 per cent. See Marx, *Capital*, vol. 3, p. 150. In volume 1 he is explicit: '. . . apart from . . . relative differences of the value of money in different countries, the wage in the first nation (in context this clearly means the more developed) is higher than in the second (the less developed), whilst the relative price of labour, i.e. the price of labour as compared with surplus value and with the value of the product, stands higher in the second than in the first' (Marx, *Capital*, vol. 1, p. 572). Charles Bettelheim, who cites this passage, adds his own emphatic comment: 'In other words, *the more productive forces are developed, the more the proletarians are exploited*, that is the higher the proportion of surplus labour to necessary labour. This is *one of the fundamental laws of the capitalist mode of production*. Reciprocally, of course, this means that, despite their low wages, the workers of the underdeveloped countries are *less exploited* than those of the advanced and so dominant countries'. See Arghiri Emmanuel, *Unequal Exchange* (London: New Left Books, 1972); Appendix I, Theoretical Comments by Charles Bettelheim, p. 302.

the same in the other? If we duck the question by arguing the rate of exploitation is higher in the underdeveloped countries because real wages are lower, we immediately throw out the law of value and surrender to neo-classical economics which can make mincemeat of this argument. If we square up to it, we have to face the unpalatable fact that capitalism has created underdevelopment not simply because it has exploited the underdeveloped countries but because it has not exploited them enough.

3. The Accumulation of Capital

In capitalist society reproduction takes place on an ever-extending scale. The social product always exceeds necessary consumption: as it does in every class society. But capitalism differs from other class societies in one vital respect: the surplus takes the form of surplus value, is appropriated by capital as profit and systematically ploughed back into production, for it is the nature of capital to expand. 'Accumulate, accumulate! That is Moses and the Prophets. Accumulation for accumulation's sake, production for production's sake ...'[1]

1. *The pursuit of pure quantity*

Accumulation can best be understood by contrasting it with collecting and hoarding.

Genuine collectors amass the objects of their choice on the basis of attraction alone. Some are drawn to natural objects such as stones, shells or leaves; others find satisfaction in man-made products like books, stamps or paintings. Either way it is the nature of what is collected that defines the collection: i.e. a collection of shells, or a collection of books. In fact, one can talk of a collection without any reference to its size. Imagine a bibliophile with £100 to spend on his collection. If he were interested primarily in its size he would buy crate-loads of second-hand paper-backs and if he got them at 5p a piece he could add 2000 to his shelves. But the genuine bibliophile would have some more serious criteria – subject matter, binding, print and so on. He might buy only 20 books with his £100, or a single rare edition. In the case of collecting, quantity is strictly subordinate to quality: with accumulation the relationship is reversed.

For this reason accumulation appears much closer to hoarding and, in fact, the two are often confused with each other. Both involve the amassing of wealth with the primary emphasis

[1] Marx, *Capital*, vol. 1, p. 606.

on quantity. To both the miser who hoards and the capitalist who accumulates the important questions are, how much? and how quickly? But there is an important difference between them. Hoarding involves extracting wealth from circulation and putting it in cold storage with the result that it cannot be employed to acquire more. It is the *passive* amassing of wealth. Accumulation, on the other hand, does not anaesthetise wealth in this way. No sooner is it drawn out of circulation than it is thrown back in again to breed and multiply. In contradistinction, therefore, to hoarding, accumulation involves an active emphasis on the quantitative aspect of wealth: in short it is the active pursuit of pure quantity. As such it is never ending, self-justifying and relentless. From every human perspective it is utterly absurd.

Parallel to the distinction between accumulation on the one hand and collecting and hoarding on the other, it is necessary to distinguish between two types of saving, for confusion about the nature of accumulation can easily arise from this quarter. It is obvious that saving (i.e. non-consumption) is a necessary condition for accumulation, since what is consumed and used up cannot be retained and accumulated. At the same time, saving does not necessarily imply accumulation. Some saving is merely a deferment of consumption, for example that of the working class. For instance, setting aside part of family income during the winter to pay for a summer holiday, or putting aside money for old age is merely a postponement of consumption. This type of saving is quite different in principle from that which fuels accumulation, for it involves only a temporary postponement of consumption not permanent abstention. In practice these two types of saving are difficult to distinguish, and frequently that saving, which for the individuals who undertake is of the one type, acts from the point of view of the economy as a whole, as the other. A simple example shows why.

Let us consider saving for old age which is clearly a deferment of consumption. Assume a working class population of 1 mn which is paid each year a social wage of £200 mn. As part of this population will be over retirement age, a proportion of the social wage will be paid out in the form of pensions. The age distribution of the population and the allocation fo the social wage can take the following form:

	£mn
800,000 active workers with an average wage of £225 per annum	£180
200,000 retired workers with an average pension of £100 per annum	20
social wage	£200

Now assume that the retired workers are able to supplement their pensions by an average of £30 out of previous savings, so that their average expenditure is £130 per annum. This means an annual dissaving of £6 mn. At the same time assume that active workers each save, on average, £25 of their income in anticipation of old age: this adds up to an annual saving of £20 mn. Subtracting the first sum from the second we are left with annual net saving of £14 mn, which is always present as a permanent fund for accumulation despite the fact that individuals save only on a temporary basis.

When we say that working class saving, or for that matter all saving, is a deferment of consumption, we are examining the phenomenon from the point of view of the individual. The individual saves so that he may spend later, but these individual actions are transformed by the social conditions in which they take place. In our example, one group of individuals saves while another group dissaves, but the *net* effect of all these actions is to create a permanent pool of savings which exists independently and can be used for purposes that never entered into their calculations.

The relationship between saving and accumulation is further complicated by the fact that all savings, even those which are only a temporary deferment of consumption, tend to grow in capitalist society. From this, it is mistakenly concluded that the purpose of all saving is the postponement of present consumption in return for increased consumption in the future. Even that saving which is done solely as a safeguard against a future drop in income or some unforeseen emergency, is invariably deposited in a form that yields a return. Few people store their savings away in a private hiding place where they are exposed to the dangers of theft and inflation, when they can be placed in a bank or used to purchase an insurance policy, which not only guarantees safety but also provides some interest on the principal. Further, the argument continues, this additional consumption and rationale for saving, can only be realised if production expands to make more goods available. But this is no problem because saving itself provides the resources for expanded production. The logic of this argument is not incorrect in itself, but the conclusions often drawn from it, that increased consumption is the mainspring of accumulation, misses the point completely. For, to begin with, it can only operate within the framework of capitalist society where accumulation is already established as an *objective* feature of social existence.

Contrast saving in capitalist society with saving in a primitive agrarian community where most production is for the immediate use of its direct producers and savings usually take the form of a part of the crop. Most peasants save part of a good harvest to help out in lean years to come, and like working class saving this is simply a rephasing of consumption. But the peasant has no choice over the use of his savings; all he can do is to store them. He cannot deposit them in a bank, nor take an insurance policy; he cannot use them in a way that will yield him a higher level of consumption in the future. These options are open to a worker in capitalist society but only because he lives in capitalist society. It is the existence of accumulation in capitalist society that makes possible a higher level of consumption in return for saving, and not the prospect of higher consumption that leads first to saving and then accumulation.

Yet this is how the relationship between consumption, saving and accumulation appears when it is studied from the point of view of the individual. From this standpoint accumulation shows up as the consequence of individual actions and not as an objective social process that determines these actions. In other words, the relationship between consumption saving and accumulation, seen through the eyes of an individual, appears exactly the reverse of what it is in practice. Furthermore the real nature of accumulation is obscured and the whole of capitalist production is given a false rationalisation.

Although neo-classical economists generally begin their analyses from the point of view of the individual and thereby achieve with unfailing regularity a totally inverted picture of reality, the reluctance to treat accumulation as an objective social process which exists independently of individual actions, and, in fact, controls these actions, is not restricted to them alone. The chief reason for this is not hard to discover. Accumulation, as the pursuit of pure quantity, is utterly irrational in individual or social terms. Setting aside part of the product of society to produce more goods that are wanted makes perfect sense in human terms, and the abstinence it involves is not difficult to justify. But setting aside part of the product for the sole purpose of increasing production, where increased consumption is purely incidental to the business in hand; in short, abstinence for accumulation is an absurd perversion of the process. This, however, is what really does take place in capitalist society.

Social processes do not arise out of men's motives; on the contrary they shape and determine these motives. The desire for increased consumption as it exists in capitalist society, and the justification it offers for saving, is a consequence of accumulation and not its origin. On the one hand accumulation creates the moral climate in which increased consumption becomes a generally accepted goal; on the other it provides the additional output that makes increased consumption possible. At all times it is accumulation that sets the pace and through their individual drive to increase consumption men achieve an end that is no part of their purpose. 'They make their own history, but they do not make it just as they please; they do not make it under circumstances chosen by themselves, but under circumstances directly encountered [and] given . . .'[2]

2. *Accumulation and money*

In order that accumulation as the pursuit of pure quantity may become an established social practice, it is necessary for the quantitative aspect of wealth to assume an independent social existence. The most elementary reason for this is practical. If not the quantitative aspect of products cannot be separated from the products themselves, accumulation can only take place through building up physical stocks. In some societies wealth

---

[2] Marx, '*The Eighteenth Brumaire of Louis Bonaparte*', Marx and Engels, *Selected Works*, vol. 1 (Moscow: Foreign Languages Publishing House, 1962), p. 247.

has been held in this direct material way, for example, as cattle. But it is not conducive to accumulation. Firstly, it involves costs: cattle have to be fed and tended; while other products which have made up stocks of wealth at various times such as corn and fabrics, tend to deteriorate. Secondly, it is inflexible. Wealth in a fixed material form is suitable for misers who hoard but not capitalists who accumulate.

What is the quantitative aspect of wealth? and in what form can it achieve an independent social existence?

In all societies wealth is finally reducible to a stock of material products, but even in the most primitive community this stock comprises different items. In advanced societies the range of different products becomes extremely wide, but the problem of quantifying wealth would exist if there were only two products, for the reason that items that are qualitatively different from each other cannot be added together directly. It is possible to add 10 tons of corn to 5 tons of corn and arrive at a meaningful total of 15 tons of corn; but 10 tons of corn cannot be added to 5 cars in the same way. On the other hand, to deny the existence of a quantitative aspect of wealth on the grounds that it cannot be measured directly would be absurd. However, we have already seen the solution to this problem. It is possible to bring different material products together into a quantitative relationship with each other since they have one qualitative property in common: they are all the products of human labour and as such they all possess value. Moreover, they all contain value in definite amounts, depending upon the amount of labour that is socially necessary for their production. Thus it is the magnitude of value which is the quantitative aspect of wealth. This is true of all wealth in all forms of society; but it is only under special conditions that it achieves an independent social expression.

If we consider the individual product in isolation, it is clear that in so far as it is the product of a definite amount of labour it possesses a definite amount of value. But if it is consumed directly by those who produce it, this will never achieve a clear social expression. Where there are two products, and moreover where they are exchanged for each other, matters are quite different, and their value aspect is brought to the fore. While the immediate purpose of a barter is to exchange one use-value for another, and for this reason the two products must be materially different from each other, it can only take place as a quantitative relation (i.e. 1 coat = 2 pairs of shoes) because the two products being exchanged share a common property–value. This does not mean that the exchange ratio of the products is exactly equal to that of their values; only, that in order to be exchangeable at all both must possess value. When products become commodities and exchange is systematic, the magnitude of value figures as one of the most prominent features of social life, only it does not do so directly in its own right, but as exchange-value.

We have seen that a commodity is different from a product in so far as it serves as an object of exchange and that it is produced with this fact in mind. In other words, the commodity, in addition to being a use-value and a receptacle of value, is also an exchange-value. And it is in this role that its property of possessing value, and moreover of possessing it in definite amounts, is made apparent. It must be emphasised yet again that this does not mean that the rate at which individual commodities exchange for each other in practice, i.e. their prices, is strictly determined by their values: all it reveals is that as the products of labour they possess value.

Thus it is under commodity production that the magnitude of value, that is the quantitative aspect of wealth, becomes an explicit feature of economic and social life. Furthermore, it is under this form of production that it achieves an independent social expression. The transformation of products into commodities and the establishment of exchange as a systematic and permanent feature of economic life, creates the need and the possibility for a specialised medium of exchange, that is *money*. Since all commodities exchange for money, money must relate to their common quality, i.e. their value. But it relates to it in a quantitative way, and however imperfect it might be as a measure of value, money nevertheless is its measure and it is socially recognised as such. As a result in a society based upon commodity production, where money exists as an established medium of exchange, it is not necessary to hold wealth in a physical form; it can now be held as money. And in this form the two disadvantages we mentioned earlier are overcome: wealth held in the form of money is neither costly to maintain nor inflexible in use. The development of money is thus a main pre-condition for systematic accumulation.

Money relates to accumulation in another less direct but not less important way: like accumulation it is purely quantitative. It cannot be consumed and in itself it has no use-value: it is pure exchange-value and as such pure quantity. One sum of money can differ from another only in respect of its size. As the independent expression of the quantitative aspect of wealth, money, therefore, already implies accumulation. Thus we can trace the roots of accumulation back beyond the existence of capital to money, and as the existence of money depends upon commodity production, we can trace it further back to the commodity itself. In other words the seed of capital accumulation lies outside capital society altogether and it must be tracked down to its origins in simple commodity production.

3. *Accumulation and simple commodity production*

Consider a society based upon simple commodity production in which all producers are independent in the sense that they own their means of production. In such a society labour-power is not a commodity and therefore industrial capital does not exist at all. Nevertheless in this form of society all the elements of capitalism including its class structure and accumulation are already present, albeit in a rudimentary form. Simple commodity production is the laboratory in which we can study the genesis of capital accumulation.

Since they own their means of production the producers are independent in the sense that they can realise their labour directly in a commodity which is their own private property. On the other hand they are not self-sufficient. Commodity production takes place only when there is an established market for the exchange of different commodities and this in turn presupposes a definite development of the division of labour. So although the individual producer is independent in the sense that he does not have to sell his labour-power, he is dependent upon other producers in so far as he does not produce everything he needs. Some items he produces for himself; others he can only acquire through exchange. He sells the commodities he produces but cannot use, and buys in return those commodities of other producers which he needs. This activity can be represented by the simple circuit:

$$C - M - C'$$

Selling in order to buy: the first leg of the circuit, $C - M$, represents the act of selling; the second $M - C'$, that of buying. As the circuit opens and closes with a commodity in the form of a use-value it is clear that its primary aspect is qualitative. The producer is chiefly concerned with exchanging one use-value for another.

In every society the basic process of social reproduction must take place and the circuit $P \dots Cn$ must be present in one form or another. In this society it works through the circuit of the independent producer in the following way:

$$P \dots C - M - C' \dots Cn$$

The commodities which are taken to market must first be produced $(P \dots C)$, while those that are purchased are acquired for consumption, both personal and productive $(C' \dots Cn)$. But as the circuit of the producer must pass through the market, so the poles of the circuit of social reproduction can only be linked by exchange. Buying and selling become indispensable economic activities and once this happens the conditions are present for the emergence of capital, initially in the form of merchant capital. Selling in order to buy, both logically and in practice, implies its reverse: buying in order to sell. The circuit of the producer, $C - M - C'$, implies the circuit of the merchant, $M - C - M'$, which is also the characteristic form of the circuit of capital.

In the first instance the development of the practice of buying in order to sell appears as a simple extension of the division of labour. A society based entirely upon commodity production, where every member of the population is dependent upon exchange for at least a part of his necessary consumption, requires that each year a certain amount of labour time is devoted to commercial activities. At first this may be undertaken by the individual producers themselves who take their own wares to market and organise all the necessary transactions. However, this can never be more than a stop-gap arrangement. For as the division of labour advances the scale and complexity of trade grows. For example, the amount of labour time it requires in a society where producers are largely self-sufficient and exchange, say, only 10 per cent of their output, is much less than in a more specialised society where, say, 90 per cent of output passes through the market. Thus if producers were forced to handle all market transactions themselves with each one seeking out customers for his products and finding suppliers for his own needs, chaos would soon prevail and every further development of production would make matters worse rather than better. But as in so many other areas of life, the creation of a problem also defines its solution. The creation of commercial disorder by the advance of the division of labour is no exception, and the problem it poses can be solved by the application of the division of labour to commercial activities themselves. Instead of handling all the trade themselves, producers grow to rely upon the services of specialised merchants who do this work for them. Thus the circuit $C - M - C'$ implies its reverse $M - C - M'$ in a very direct and obvious way. But what starts out as a simple extension of the division of labour, a development which in the first instance is primarily technical, soon hardens into a *social* division of labour that pre-figures the class divisions of capitalist society in many important respects.

The first function of the market is to facilitate the social distribution of commodities as use-values, allowing producers to exchange these commodities which have no direct use to them for others which they can use. And the first function of trading as a specialised form of social labour is to facilitate this process and economise on the amount of social labour time it requires. In the process it becomes indispensable to the whole structure of commodity production itself for as the following circuit shows it not only mediates between the producers but becomes a vital link between the two poles of the circuit of social reproduction.

$$P \ldots C - (M - C - M') - C' \ldots Cn$$

In a shorthand way this circuit defines the link. Its essential structure is that of the circuit of social reproduction as it exists in a commodity-producing society. It starts with production and ends with consumption. The producer takes his product to market $(C - M)$ and buys the items he wants $(M - C')$. But neither of these transactions takes place directly with other producers like himself: both are conducted with merchants. The merchant buys the commodities of one producer $(M - C)$ which he then sells to another $(C - M')$ so at the heart of the circuit of social reproduction the trading activities this circuit represents still involve the social distribution of commodities. At the same time, trading is a specialised form of activity and within this general context it has its own individual specifications. Although buying in order to sell is dependent upon the fundamental processes of production and consumption, and is ultimately subordinate to them, it nevertheless possesses its own logic and rationality, which is simply the pursuit of pure quantity. For anyone whose economic activity takes this form and can be described by the circuit $M - C - M'$ must inevitably be governed by the logic of pure gain. Whatever the wider implications of this circuit might be, its immediate purpose is unmistakable. The merchant is in business to make money. If at the end of the day M' just equals M he has wasted his time, if it is less he has wasted his money.

The characteristic feature of the commodity is that quantitative aspect of wealth, value, achieves an independent social existence which is separate from its material being as use-value. In a society based upon commodity production this separation expresses itself in the form of two distinct classes whose economic activities are characterised by two opposed circuits. On the side of use-value is the producer with his circuit $C - M - C'$: on that of value, the merchant with his circuit, $M - C - M'$. In other words the internal division of the commodity is now concretely expressed in the division of society into two classes: one producing use-values and exchanging them for other use-values; the other engaging in no other activity but exchange for its own sake. Thus the principle of accumulation already inherent in the commodity, becomes, in a society based upon commodity production, the sole and defining practice of a distinct social class. For this type of society where the quantitative aspect of production has a socially independent form of being, there exists a corresponding class whose economic activity relates exclusively to this aspect of production and whole sole reason for existence is accumulation.

Merchant's wealth is always capital. The form it assumes at any moment is temporary and always the premise for another.

Thus the merchant turns his money into commodities which he resells as quickly as he can; and no sooner has he returned his wealth to money than he is looking for more commodities to buy:

$$M - C - M' - C - M''\ldots$$

So it is with the industrial capitalist. He turns his money into commodities that are means of production to produce other commodities to sell and reconvert into money. But this is not a final resting point, or even a base from which he can enjoy the fruits of other people's labour: it is premise for doing the same thing all over again on a larger scale.

$$M - C^L_{MP}\ldots P \ldots C' - M' - C^L_{MP}\ldots P \ldots C - M''\ldots$$

The defining characteristic of wealth when it becomes capital is that no one form is an end in itself, but a prelude to another. And this can mean only one thing: the capitalist as capitalist, that is as the representative of capital, is not interested in particular forms of wealth, but in wealth in general; not interested in the particular features of one form of wealth, but in the common property of all wealth. He is concerned solely with wealth as *value*.

The circuit of capital, both merchant capital and industrial capital, is thus a continuous movement from one form of value to another. But value, we know, has no qualitative distinguishing features. As an object of value commodities, or money, are qualitatively all the same: they are all the products of the same abstract labour. In only one respect can they differ – size: one commodity can embody more or less value than another; but otherwise the two are identical. Thus from the point of view of value the only logical reason for switching from one commodity to another, or from one form of wealth to another, as capital does all the time, is purely quantitative. The circuit of capital then is nothing other than value in motion and for this reason can have no other rationality than the pursuit of pure quantity. In a word capital is the social incarnation of accumulation.

4. *Commodity production and capitalism*

In capitalist society proper all the barriers to accumulation are broken down, but industrial capitalism, as we know it today, is neither historically nor logically its starting point. Accumulation as a principle is present in the commodity, and capital as its objective social expression appears as soon as commodity production expands to a point that permits the emergence of a class of specialised merchants. Historically the transition from commodity production and merchant capital, to capitalist production and industrial capital, was a lengthy and complex process which was far from uniform in different parts of the world. We shall see that it took a very different form in the developed and underdeveloped countries which largely accounts for the present division of the world. At this stage, however, we are concerned with the transition in logical terms alone, where it is a relatively short and simple step. A comparison of the basic circuits that characterise economic activity in the two situations quickly shows that: (1) capitalist production is only a special form of commodity production; but, (2) it is its highest form.

The fundamental similarities of the two modes of production is revealed by the structural features their basic circuits have in common. Contrast, for example, the circuit of the independent commodity producer

$$C - M - C'$$

with that of the wage labourer

$$L \ldots P \ldots - m - c$$

In both the structure of exchange is identical, beginning and ending with a commodity in its material form, thereby emphasising the qualitative purpose of the transaction in both cases: the exchange of one use-value for another which is different. The same type of similarity is to be found between the circuit of merchant capital

$$M - C - M'$$

and the circuit of industrial capital

$$M - C^L_{MP} \ldots P \ldots C' - M'$$

as both are a complete inversion of the two above. They both begin and end with money which shows that the acquisition of quantity, accumulation, is their primary purpose. Both modes of production, therefore, are characterised by two basic circuits each of which is the exact opposite of the other. Moreover, in both situations the activity of each class is dependent upon the other and their circuits combine with each other. In the case of simple commodity production this combined circuit takes the following form:

$$C - (M - C - M') - C'$$

while in capitalist society it is rather more complex:

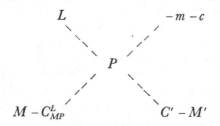

Nevertheless the similarities are unmistakable: in both cases the circuit of the direct producers, on the one hand the independent producers and on the other the wage-labourers, are interrupted by the circuit of capital. Neither one is able to gain access to his means of consumption without engaging in some form of transaction with capital. The necessity of this transaction defines the structural similarities of the two modes of production: its different nature is their point of divergence.

Under simple commodity production the producer meets the merchant, the representative of capital, in a purely trading context, selling him his own commodities on the one hand $(C - M)$, and on the other buying from him the commodities of other producers $(M - C')$. In capitalist society the two classes also trade with each other when the workers buy their means of consumption $(m - c)$ from the capitalists $(C - M')$ at the end of their respective circuits. Moreover, each circuit opens with an act of exchange, the worker selling his labour-power $(L - m)$ and the capitalist purchasing it $(M - C^L)$. But this is an exchange with a difference. When the independent producer sells his commodity, he is literally finished with it: it is a final commodity which has already passed through the process of production. Moreover the commodity varies from one producer to the next. In capitalist society, on the other hand, the wage-labourer always sells the same commodity, labour-power, and it is not a final commodity at all. The shoes or the coat or whatever it might be that the independent producer takes to market can fulfil its role as a use-value without any further effort on his part; but not so with labour-power. This commodity which the capitalist buys can only realise its use-value when it is employed in productive activity, that is when the labourer is set to work in a manner laid down and supervised by the capitalist. The buying and selling of labour-power is therefore not at all a simple transaction whereby a use-value is exchanged for money and matters end: it requires the seller to submit himself to the direct control of the buyer for the transaction to have any meaning at all.

The whole difference between simple commodity and capitalist production pivots on this single point. In both cases the circuit of the direct producer must pass through the circuit of capital: but whereas the circuits of the independent producer and merchant capital intersect only in the market, those of the wage-labourer and the industrial capitalist *converge* in the sphere of production. As this takes place, capital rips off the fetters that previously bound it, and by seizing control of productions it not only transforms the independent producer into a proletarian, but releases itself from all the constraints that previously restricted its drive to accumulate.

For production is the key to accumulation since the profits of all capital, even merchant capital that operates exclusively in the sphere of circulation, originate in the sphere of production.[3] They come out of surplus production, but it does not follow from this that they equal surplus production. On the contrary, one of the main restrictions on the rate of accumulation of merchant capital is that it can only appropriate a proportion of the surplus, and is unable to prevent other classes taking a share. Thus the first task of industrial capital is to increase its share, that is to transform a greater part of surplus production into surplus value. In the theoretical conditions of simple commodity production this means depriving the independent producers of part of their income which becomes progressively easier as they lose their independence and are reduced to a proletarian status. For the power of capital *vis-à-vis* the direct producers of wealth increases as it employs them directly and relies less and less on trade as a means of

[3] See below, pp. 86–9.

acquiring profits. In the first instance, industrial capital takes the world as it finds it with respect to technology and markets, for its new-found power is sufficient initially for it to shift the distribution of income in its favour and thereby increase its rate of accumulation.

But the advantages it wins in this way cannot suffice over the long period. The rate of accumulation, we have seen, depends not simply on the absolute amount of surplus value and profit, but on surplus value relative to the total capital advanced in its acquisition; namely the rate of profit. Thus as capital accumulates and its value increases, any given rate of accumulation demands a growth in the absolute amount of surplus value and profit. For example, assume a capital whose initial value, M, equals 100, which gains a surplus value and profit of 20, so that its second value, M', rises to 120. In this case its rate of profit $(M' - M)/M$ equals 20 per cent, which is also the rate at which it can accumulate. In other words it can open its second circuit with a capital 20 per cent greater than that which opened it first. To maintain this rate of expansion its rate of profit in this circuit must also equal 20 per cent, i.e. $(M'' - M')/M$ must equal 20 per cent. As M' equals 120, M'' must equal 144. In other words surplus value and profit must rise from 20 to 24, i.e. by 20 per cent, in order for accumulation to continue at the same rate. This holds as a general rule: for any given rate of accumulation to be maintained through time, the absolute amount of surplus value and profit must grow. But once all surplus production has been transformed into surplus value the rate of accumulation must fall unless capital can find a new way to increase it. The only method open to it is also the most revolutionary for it involves increasing the mass of social production itself, not just once but continuously. At this moment 'accumulation for accumulation's sake' becomes 'production for production's sake'.

Assuming that all surplus production is appropriated by capital as surplus value, an increase in the mass of production can increase absolute surplus value in two ways. Firstly, in so far as necessary consumption remains a constant part of social output, it rises proportionately with the growth in output. Thus if necessary consumption requires 80 per cent of annual production, a doubling of production from, say, 100 to 200, doubles surplus value from 20 to 40. Secondly, it can rise even faster than this. If at the same time as production doubles from 100 to 200, necessary consumption falls from 80 to 60 per cent of output, surplus value increases fourfold from 20 to 80. This is what tends to happen in practice.

As production can grow continuously over any substantial period of time only so long as the productivity of labour rises, a rise in output must be accompanied by a general fall in the value of commodities, and in particular, a fall in the value of labour-power. In Chapter 4 we saw the implications of this fall; how it made possible a rise in real wages at the same time as a fall in the value of wages. From the point of view of accumulation it is the value of wages that is significant, for as this drops the proportion of social production going to labour falls while that passing to capital as surplus value rises. In this way the survival of capital as the social incarnation of accumulation becomes identified with the growth of output, and capital is launched upon its historic mission to develop and socialise the forces of production.

5. *Accumulation and the socialisation of labour*

The basis for any sustained rise in production and productivity is the development of the division of labour. To begin with the growth of specialisation need not involve fundamental changes in the methods of production. In Adam Smith's pin factory, to take the most famous example,[4] the dramatic rise in productivity arose entirely from the reorganisation of the productive process. No new techniques were adopted. Pin-making, Adam Smith observed, required eighteen separate processes such as drawing out the wire, straightening, cutting, pointing and grinding it, and so on. When ten men performed all these processes individually they could never produce more than 200 pins among them in a day. But when each man specialised on one or two of these processes, production rose dramatically to 48,000 pins. The division of labour is not, of course, specific to capitalist society, but it has been most fully developed under capitalism where it has assumed a particular social significance.

Labour is always inherently social even where the process of

---

[4] Adam Smith, *The Wealth of Nations*, vol. 1, 6th ed. (London: Methuen, 1961), pp. 8–9.

production is organised around individuals, as is the case with simple commodity production. However, here it can only achieve indirect expression in the sphere of circulation when men take their goods to market. Removed from its real theatre in the sphere of production it often appears as a social relationship between things rather than between the men that produce them. On the other hand it is true to say that in rural societies, where conditions very roughly approximate those of simple commodity production, market day was the most important event in the social calendar. In capitalist society where the factory becomes the unit of production and the accumulation of capital leads to a continuous extension of the division of labour, the social nature of labour achieves a direct expression in the sphere of production and becomes an immediate aspect of working class life all day and every day.

This is already apparent in the relatively primitive conditions of Adam Smith's pin factory. After the reorganisation of production on the basis of specialisation ten workers are able to produce 48,000 pins, compared with the maximum of 200 they could previously make when working individually. So the daily output of the individual worker rises from 20 pins to 4800. The simplicity of this calculation, however, and the dramatic increase in productivity which it measures, obscures a most important fact; namely, that the term 'the individual worker' has changed its significance. Where each worker produces alone, it is meaningful to talk of individual output, for it is indeed the output of an individual worker. Or to look at the matter in a different way, we can calculate the output of the ten separate workers in the unspecialised pin factory by adding together the number of pins that each produces. But we cannot make this calculation after the reorganisation of production. For production has become a collective activity which means that no worker any longer makes anything by himself. The term 'the individual worker' no longer refers to a particular individual; it is a numerical abstraction arrived at by dividing the total labour force by the number of workers who comprise it. From the real and productive point of view, the individual worker is replaced by the collective worker in which the individual has become merely a component part. In other words the individual can only act as a producer if he becomes a member of a collective labour force; if he submerges his individuality into this collective. 'When numerous labourers work together side by side . . . (in this way) . . . they are said to co-operate, or to work in *co-operation*.'[5]

Even in the early days of capitalist production co-operation was not restricted to the single factory and as production develops it expands to embrace more and more of the economy. Consider a modern car factory. Clearly co-operation exists within the factory where car production is not undertaken by the aggregated efforts of individuals working separately, but by the collective effort of a mass of workers who form a single labour force. But car production is not an isolated activity that takes place only in particular factories whose final product is cars: it also needs the production of coal and steel, and all the other materials that enter into the fabric of the automobile. And the collective efforts of the mass of workers in these other branches of production are as much a part of car manufacture as that of the workers on the final conveyor belt. In other words, the collectivity of labour extends beyond the single plant and embraces the full circuit of material production. As different branches of production are drawn together in this way and co-operation spreads throughout the whole economy, we can say that production has become *socialised* in the sense that no one branch of production can function in isolation from the general productive activities of society as a whole.

The extension of the division of labour, co-operation and the socialisation of production are, in the first instance, aspects of material production and therefore not peculiar to any one mode of production. On the other hand, they develop most rapidly in capitalist society where the inherent drive of capital to accumulate forces it to expand production continuously in its effort to increase surplus value both relatively and absolutely. Or to put the matter another way, they are developed most rapidly in capitalist society but for the purposes of accumulation and not for their own sake. Consequently they are distorted and prevented from realising their full potential. Just as capital is forced to produce use-values in order to produce value, so it must socialise labour and production in order to accumulate. The distortion this brings to the process of socialisation is

[5] Marx, *Capital*, vol. 1, p. 315.

strictly analogous to that of the production of use-values which arises from the subordination of material to value production: production for profit rather than need – cars instead of public transport; office space instead of housing and so on. In fact it is nothing more than the dynamic expression of the fundamental human illogicality of capitalist production.

The full implications of the subordination of material production to value production are not apparent at the relatively low levels of material production that characterise the early phases of capitalist development. When social output is relatively low and necessary consumption absorbs a large part of it, the immediate material requirements of social reproduction exercise a decisive influence of production – i.e. the bulk of production must be devoted to basic items of personal consumption. In this context the process of accumulation can appear as an effort to expand production for the sake of increased consumption. But as production expands under the impetus of accumulation and the proportion of it required for necessary consumption falls, the material requirements of social reproduction no longer exert the same decisive influence upon it. Capital gains much greater room for manœuvre and as the value aspect of production comes to the fore the real nature of accumulation as the pursuit of pure quantity is revealed. But not to the representatives of capital: what class could ever recognise that its social practice is utterly absurd in human terms? It is left to labour, the real basis of accumulation for whom the socialisation of production is an immediate experience of life, to grasp the true nature of the situation and transform it to one that has a genuine human significance. But this transformation is not automatic. Not only is it dependent upon political relations which are never the simple analogue of economic relations, but the drive to achieve it can be outflanked for some time at least if not indefinitely, by capital which turns the struggle to overthrow it into a motor of its own development. As this happens capital itself becomes socialised.

6. *Accumulation and the socialisation of capital*

Capital, we have seen, takes the world very much as it finds it, and the development of the forces of production at the start of industrial capitalism in Britain at the end of the eighteenth century, were such that production could be effectively organ- ised in fairly small factories owned and run independently. But as production develops two things start to happen. Firstly, the scale of production in the successful firms increases. And, to the extent that this gives rise to economies of scale, it increases faster than production as a whole leading to a reduction in their number. This is called the *concentration* of capital and has received much attention from orthodox and other economists alike. Secondly, different branches of production become more closely integrated with each other in an immediate and direct way. At first, this can be handled through the normal channels of commodity circulation with firms buying and selling to each other the various materials and machinery that are indispens- able for their operations. But as concentration and integration develop under the relentless pressure of accumulation these mechanisms prove less and less adequate. The vast amount of complex machinery that a car factory needs when it retools, cannot be purchased on the open market in the same way as spinning machines and looms could be acquired by textile firms at an earlier epoch of capitalist development. Special arrange- ments are necessary in this field. They are also necessary in the field of material supplies, for firms that have sunk a large am- ount of capital in equipment would face serious losses if they could not guarantee a steady flow of these materials.[6] In addition some types of material undertaking, such as the construction of nuclear power stations, are too large to be undertaken by single firms. For all these reasons the market is gradually supplemented as the sinew by more direct methods of integration. Different firms collaborate with each other, set up consortia or merge to form much larger units. This is called the *centralisation* of capital.

Concentration and centralisation go together hand in hand as two aspects of the same process – the socialisation of capital which is a necessary part of the socialisation of production in capitalist society. The development of co-operation is one side of the coin; they are the other. Each is the premise of the other, and at the same time a response to it: the growth of co-operation is fostered by concentration and centralisation; equally concen-

[6] See J. K. Galbraith, *The New Industrial State* (London: Penguin, 1969).

tration and centralisation make an increase in the scale of co-operation possible. However, it must never be forgotten that both have a single origin; the growth in the scale of material production which accumulation establishes as a permanent structural feature of capitalist society.

The development of capital from its first beginnings as merchant capital through to monopoly capital and beyond, is the unfolding of its basic nature. The socialisation of capital is always inherent in capital whatever its stage of development, in the way that the flower is inherent in the seed from which it springs; though of course it depends upon propitious conditions for its realisation – a flower cannot bloom if the soil is barren and the climate hostile. The transition from merchant to industrial capital constitutes a systematisation of the process of accumulation. It is a step which allows capital to realise its nature as capital more fully than before. So it is with the concentration and centralisation of capital. Far from being a deviation from the norm of competition – often mistakenly identified as the very essence of capital and the real source of accumulation[7] – they are modifications in its organisation which allow it to accumulate more effectively.

7 Kidron speaks for many people when he writes '. . . the relations between different capitals are by and large competitive; . . . and an individual capital's competitive strength is more or less related to the size and scope of its operations. . . . Were it not . . . [so] . . . there would be no compulsion on each capital to grow as fast as it might through "accumulation" . . . and "concentration" '. Michael Kidron, *Western Capitalism since the War* (Penguin Books, 1970), p. 48. Baron and Sweezy, who seem well aware that the mainsprings of accumulation are to be found in the nature of capital: 'The heart and care of the capitalist function is accumulation: accumulation has always been the prime mover of the system' (p. 55), nevertheless assert 'the Marxian analysis of capitalism still rests in the final analysis as the assumption of a competitive economy'. Paul Baron and Paul Sweezy, *Monopoly Capital* (London: Penguin Books, 1968), p. 17. If one wished to make out a strong case for the importance of competition in Marx's work, it could best be done on the question of the means by which a general rate of profit is established. Chapter 10 of *Capital*, vol. 3 is indeed entitled 'Equalisation of the General Rate of Profit Through Competition'. But the whole spirit of the analysis here puts competition very firmly into second place. 'For . . . the average rate of profit', Marx writes, 'depends upon the intensity of exploitation of the sum of total labour by the sum of total capital' (p. 197). In other words, competition comes into play only after surplus value has been produced. Moreover, for this reason, individual capitalists become

We can look at this matter from a different angle. Even where capital consists of a whole number of independent firms that compete with each other, it is still meaningful to talk of social capital which has a distinct social existence *vis-à-vis* labour upon whose exploitation every independent capitalist depends. But in its competitive phase the social nature of capital exists only in an abstract form in the sense that it has only a poorly developed organisational framework. The competitive structure of capital lays greater stress upon the interests of the individual capitalist to the detriment of their general interests. It is true that the state represents these general interests and will if necessary defend them against individual firms, but the capacity of the state to fulfil its role in this field is always limited by the organisational structure of capital itself. Viewed in this light, concentration and centralisation reveal themselves as the organisational forms appropriate to social capital as such: as they take place social capital transcends its abstract nature and begins to emerge as a concrete force. This process is effected through three interrelated changes in the organisational structure of capital. Firstly, individual firms increase their scale of operations and new forms of administrative control emerge – Galbraith calls these *technostructure*. Secondly, the number of firms tends to diminish relatively if not absolutely, and competition between them is gradually replaced by some form of organised collaboration, even where this collaboration is covert and illegal. Thirdly, the state itself intervenes directly and often takes the initiative in arranging for collaboration. Economists of all schools of thought lay great stress upon these changes which it is commonly agreed mark the end of *laisser-faire*. But generally they treat them as a degeneration of capitalism from its ideal norm of competition

---

aware of their common social interests at the very moment they are competing. Hence 'they form a veritable free-mason society *vis-à-vis* the whole working class, while there is little love lost between them in competition among themselves' (p. 198). As Marx says elsewhere on this question '*the capitalists* are "communists"', *Theories of Surplus Value*, Part Three, p. 83. It is clear that the function of competition of distributing surplus value around the economy can be carried out by administrative mechanisms and that a system of regulated prices as part of a general planning policy can perform the task just as efficiently.

Galbraith sees in them the end of capitalism and the beginnings of post-capitalist society. In fact they represent a major advance for capital towards its self-realisation as a conscious and organised social force, by breaking it free of the fetters of private ownership.[8]

The first act in the rupture of the traditional property relations within which capital developed, typified by the nineteenth-century entrepreneur and captain of industry, takes place within the individual firm as the separation of ownership from control. The advent of the joint-stock company in Britain in the middle of the nineteenth century opened a rift between ownership and control which has got progressively wider. Capital was freed from the close attentions of the individual capitalist who was never a totally reliable representative of its interests, for personal frailty could always turn him to consume his profits or commit some other blasphemy against the holy grail of pure quantity. The new managerial caste that emerged as its agent is much better suited to its task. It suffers little temptation to use profits for anything other than accumulation as it has no claim over them in its role as manager. Its professional creed that commits it to abstractly defined goals such as growth, productivity and efficiency is ideally suited to the needs of capital, for they serve the objective requirements of accumulation while mystifying its true nature and thereby lifting it beyond its range of criticism. Its cultural values which stress the merits of collaborative work within a bureaucratic framework – the cultural values of the 'organisation man' – correspond to the requirements of advanced capitalism more closely than the rugged individualism of the early industrial epoch. Its

[8] With reference to the development of joint-stock companies, what we now call corporations, Marx writes, 'The capital, which in itself rests upon a social mode of production and pre-supposes a social concentration of means of production and labour-power, is here directly endowed with the form of social capital (capital of directly associated individuals) as distinct from private capital, and its undertakings assume the form of social undertakings as distinct from private undertakings. It is the abolition of capital as private property within the framework of capitalist production itself' (Marx, *Capital*, vol. 3, p. 436; see also p. 266). 'A great business is really too big to be human. It grows so large as to supplant the personality of the man. In a big business the employer like the employee is lost in the mass . . . The business itself becomes the big thing' (Henry Ford, *My Life and Work*, pp. 263–4).

growth, moreover, is not restricted to individual firms and it now dominates the administrative departments of state in most countries throughout the world. Recruited largely from the lower middle classes who have their last vestiges of independent culture and capacity for critical thought carefully removed by a vocational training that instils the utterly abstract ideals of technical progress and growth, it provides the perfect instrument of accumulation as a social process. It is, in short, the ideal representative of social capital when it 'becomes conscious of itself as a social force'.

The transition from individual to corporate capitalism that establishes this managerial caste as a force in capitalist society, does not necessarily destroy private ownership in capital. In Western countries the private ownership of the means of production has persisted alongside the development of corporate enterprise. Nevertheless the separation of ownership from control within the individual firm and the role played by the state in directing, and even planning, capitalist production, has denied it much of its former significance. To claim that private property is now a historical relic of an earlier phase of capitalist production, would perhaps, be to exaggerate the importance of what Galbraith calls the *technostructure*; on the other hand it is true to say that the personal gain of the individual capitalist is no longer the means through which the principle of accumulation achieves expression as a social force. Self-interest continues to play its part as the cultural norm that determines men's lives, but in the age of the large corporation it is more fully and more clearly subordinated to the requirements of accumulation than ever before. The capitalist class, understood in its traditional sense as the class that owned capital, is dislodged from its seat of power. The emergence of the managerial caste in the modern corporation and in the state itself shakes capital free from the capitalist. It liberates it from its midwife of private property that before the end of the nineteenth century, even, was already blocking its self-realisation as social capital.[9] In doing so it reveals as an evident fact of daily existence

---

[9] It is significant that in the nineteenth century the construction of railways which speeded the socialisation of capital more than any other single development, was not carried out by individual capitalists. In Britain, the development of railways and the emergence of new forms of capitalist

what previously could only be discovered theoretically: that capital as the social incarnation of the principle of accumulation is a relation of production and not a relation of property.

This has important implications for the class struggle.[10] Labour confronts capital not in abstract or theoretical terms, but concretely as it actually exists. This has meant that throughout most of the history of capitalism working class opposition has been directed against capital as a form of property rather than against it as a relation of production. It has fought for the expropiation of private capital and nationalisation has formed an essential plank in most working class programmes for revolutionary change. We can now see that this form of struggle, though valid in so far as it corresponded to the actual conditions in which labour found itself, did not strike at the essence of capitalist production. On the contrary, it was a force directed towards the further development of capitalism. It produced concrete demands that capital could not only concede within the existing structure of production relations, but demands whose concession led to the higher development of these relations. It exposed the working class to incorporation within the general capitalist project and turned it into one of the main motors of capitalist development.

But working class struggle is not a historical constant: both its form and content change in response to the development of capitalism. It is not that demands once satisfied, such as those for the ten-hour day, free education and full employment, lose significance with their satisfaction, however partial this satisfaction might be, but that the ongoing struggles of the class for higher wages and against conditions of exploitation are themselves changed by the development of capitalism. As the mode of production develops and capital realises itself ever more fully as a relation of production, working class struggle is continually transformed to where the most immediate and contingent forms of opposition by labour challenge the very foundations of its

---

ownership such as the joint-stock company, were intimately related. In many parts of the world, even in those supposed bastions of *laisser-faire*, the British colonies, railways were constructed by the state.

[10] It also has important implications for the transition from capitalism to communism. See note at the end of this chapter.

existence. The terrain of class struggle ceases to be any particular set of property relations but becomes capitalist production
itself. The ownership of the means of production ceases to hold
the centre of the stage as the struggle against capital is forced
by the objective conditions of its existence to become a struggle
against accumulation.

Note: Social capital and the transition to communism

The question of the transition from capitalism to a higher form
of society is now the most contentious issue in Marxist and
revolutionary thought. It is not simply a theoretical question,
for it has the most direct bearings on the strategic assessment
and articulation of class struggle in capitalist society.

Although the transition to communism has never been considered as automatic,[11] all Marxists have always agreed that
capitalism creates its pre-conditions by developing and socialis-
ing production to a point where it can no longer be contained
within the existing relations of production – capital and wage-
labour. In volume 3 of *Capital*, Marx writes:

> We have seen that the growing accumulation of capital
> implies its growing concentration. Thus grows the power of
> capital, the alienation of the conditions of social production
> personified in the capitalist from the real producers. Capital
> comes more and more to the fore as a social power, whose
> agent is the capitalist. This social power no longer stands in
> any possible relation to that which the labour of a single
> individual can create. It becomes an alienated, independent,
> social power, which stands opposed to society as an object,
> and as an object that is the capitalist's source of power. The
> contradiction between the general social power into which
> capital develops, on the one hand, and the private power of
> the individual capitalists over these social conditions of pro-
> duction, becomes ever more irreconcilable, and yet contains

[11] In the *Communist Manifesto* Marx talks of the class struggle as a 'fight
that each time ended in either a revolutionary reconstitution of society at
large – or in the common ruin of the contending classes' (Marx, *The Revolutions of 1848*, p. 68).

the solution of the problem, because it implies at the same time the transformation of the conditions of production into general common, social conditions. This transformation stems from the development of the productive forces under capitalist production, and from the ways and means by which this development takes place.[12]

The seizure of the state power by the proletariat, or by the party of the proletariat which is not necessarily the same thing, appears to be the decisive moment in this transformation. But we know that even before this political rupture takes place, capital must make accommodation for its developing social nature within the fabric of the existing society by modifying property relations. Thus long before the *dictatorship of the proletariat* is established, the means of production cease to be private property in the traditional sense. On the other side, the advent of working class political power does not in itself destroy the capitalist nature of the relations of production, which survives the earlier transformation in property relations. As Marx points out in the *Critique of the Gotha Programme*:

> What we have to deal with . . . is a communist society, not as it has *developed* on its own foundations, but on the contrary, just as it *emerges* from capitalist society; which is thus in every respect, morally and intellectually, still stamped with the birth marks of the old society from whose womb it emerges.[13]

This 'first phase of communist society' which we shall call *socialism* must be distinguished from the achievement of *communism* where

> the narrow horizon of bourgeois right [is] crossed and society inscribe[s] on its banners: From each according to his ability, to each according to his needs.[14]

Just as elements of the capitalist mode of production persist into socialist society, so elements of socialism arise in capitalist society before the achievement of state power by the proletariat.

[12] Marx, *Capital*, vol. 3, p. 264.
[13] Marx, *Critique of the Gotha Programme*, Marx and Engels. *Selected Works*. vol. 2, p. 23.
[14] Ibid. p. 24.

This poses the question of the nature of socialism. Is it a distinct mode of production? Is it a *transitional* mode of production, not just in the general sense, that all hitherto existing modes have been transitional in so far as they represent only a phase in social development and not its end, but in a specific sense? That is to say, is the structure of socialist society such, that it already contains within itself the elements of communism, which can come to the fore without the need for a further revolution? Or, to put this question yet another way, does the advent of socialism destroy the foundations of capitalism to a degree that the elements of capitalism which persist, such as money, commodity production and wage-labour, cease to have an independent social existence?

Writing in the nineteenth century when the socialisation of capital was not far advanced and before the political triumph of any working class party, Marx could only pose the problem in theoretical terms, and generally speaking, he adopted an optimistic view.

> The result of the ultimate development of capitalist production is a necessary transitional phase towards the reconversion of capital into the property of producers, although no longer as the private property of individual producers, but rather as the property of associated producers, as outright social property.[15]

Nevertheless, he does sound a warning.

> The co-operative factories of the labourers themselves represent within the old form the first sprouts of the new, although they naturally reproduce and must reproduce, everywhere in the actual organisation all the shortcomings of the prevailing system.[16]

It is true he goes on to argue that the new will triumph over the old and that their coexistence in advanced capitalism serves to 'show how a new mode of production grows out of an old one'. But, now, fifty years after the Soviet Revolution and in the light of the very profound recomposition that capital has achieved in the developed countries in the course of this century, it is

[15] Marx, *Capital*, vol. 3, p. 437.
[16] Ibid., p. 440.

surely legitimate to ask whether the balance of forces necessarily favours the new form of society, or whether the necessary tendencies of the elements of the old order to reproduce themselves within the framework of the new one, can prevail. Does socialism which certainly overcomes the traditional private property relations of capitalism, necessarily undermine the productive relations of capitalism?[17] Is it not possible for these productive relations to survive even the seizure of state power by the proletariat and reproduce themselves within the framework of the new form? In which case it is not a new form at all, but merely a further development of the old one. To put it in a nutshell: is socialism now the highest form of capitalism?[18]

[17] Certainly the view that '. . . capitalist joint stock companies . . . should be considered as transitional forms from the capitalist mode of production . . .', seems hopelessly optimistic in the light of the ability to reproduce capitalist relations of production for more than a century. Marx, *Capital*, vol. 3, p. 440.

[18] The literature on this subject is now extensive. Two works which raise many of the important issues and give extensive references are Charles Bethelheim and Paul Sweezy, *The Transition from Capitalism to Socialism* (London and New York: Monthly Review Press, 1971), and E. H. Carr, *The Bolshevik Revolution*, vol. 2 (London: Penguin Books, 1971).

roductive and Circulation Capital

It is now necessary to consider the different forms that capital assumes at different moments in its circuit. As it passes through the spheres of production and circulation so capital changes; in one it is *productive* capital; in the other *circulation* capital. These two forms are as distinct from each other as the activities to which they correspond: the production of commodities in the one case; the buying and selling of them in the other. But in capitalist society the circuit of capital does not merely embrace the spheres of production and circulation, it *unites* them: they remain distinct, but they are inseparable. So it is with the two forms of capital that operate within them: while each has its own distinguishing features, they share the common property of being capital and are governed by its general laws.

1. *Unequal exchange*

Circulation capital has played a decisive role in the history of the underdeveloped world; in particular, one type of circulation capital, *merchant capital*. We have already encountered this type of capital when we discussed simple commodity production in Chapter 3. We saw that the activities of merchants are restricted to the buying and selling of commodities. Although some merchants might undertake the transportation of commodities and others engage in some type of processing and packaging, the fundamental business of merchant capital is restricted to their exchange. Transportation and so on are not merchant activities properly speaking; they are part of the process of production which juts out into the sphere of circulation and cannot be included in the analysis of merchant capital. Or to say the same thing in a different way: there are no activities undertaken by merchant capital *qua* merchant capital which can increase the value of the commodities it handles.

The circuit of merchant capital is thus quite simply $M - C - M'$, buying in order to sell, the characteristic form of the circuit of capital. It is structurally identical to the general circuit of

capital, $M - C^L_{MP} \ldots P \ldots C' \quad M'$ in that both begin and end
with money; both involve the purchase of commodities with
their subsequent resale in mind; in both the original outlay of
money is an advance rather than an expenditure; and both
have the largest possible increase in money as their sole rationale. 'The events that take place outside the sphere of circulation, in the interval between buying and selling, do not affect
the form of this movement' from money to money.[1] The circuit
of merchant capital is thus consistent in every way with its
general nature as capital. But in one vital respect merchant
capital differs from industrial capital: whereas the latter is
able to secure the surplus product of society in the form of
surplus value and profit by exchanging all the commodities it
handles at prices equivalent to their value, merchant capital
must engage in non-equivalent or *unequal exchange*. Its circuit,
$M - C - M'$, involves two transactions but only one commodity,
and there is nothing merchant capital does to this commodity
between the moment of its purchase and subsequent sale, which
increases its value. The same commodity with the same value
features in both exchanges, so that if the two transactions took
place at value, it would be the same value. Buying price and
selling price would be equal and the merchant would make no
profit. For any profit to be made one transaction, at least, must
take place at a price that is not equal to value. This is not
simply an imperative for the individual merchant, nor an
occasional requirement that can be satisfied by the odd crooked
deal – unequal exchange is a general condition of existence for
merchant capital as a whole.

Any attempt to derive the general laws of capital from this
particular type of circulation capital, must inevitably conclude
that profit is a phenomenon of circulation, the result of buying
cheap and selling dear.[2] In other words it would appear that
the law of value does not hold. But this is not the case at all.

The profits of merchant capital appear in the first instance as

[1] Marx, *Capital*, vol. 1, p. 133.
[2] In fact, although merchant capital preceded industrial capital historically, its nature cannot be properly understood before the advent of industrial capital when it becomes clear that profit originates in the sphere of
production. In this sense science must work backwards against the stream
of history.

a sum of money $(M' - M)$ and it is in terms of money that the merchants calculate the size of their capitals. This adds to the impression that their profit is the result of exchange. But the profit of capital in general also appears first in the form of money, so merchant capital is not peculiar in this respect. Moreover, the monetary form is only one form, and it is acceptable only in so far as it can be transformed into other commodities. In other words, merchants are only prepared to conclude their transactions with a sale, $C - M'$, so long as they are confident that they can use this money to open a new circuit, $M' - C'$. Consider a double turnover of the circuit of merchant capital:

$$M - C - M' - C' - M''$$

Here the merchant ploughs back all his profit plus the amount he originally advanced (i.e. M') into trade, and we can reasonably expect that the commodities he buys with this larger sum of money are of greater value than those he originally brought, i.e. with M. In other words the value of the commodities C' is greater than that of C. If we now assume for the sake of simplicity that merchants buy at value and make their profits by selling commodities above their value, then the difference in value between these two sets of commodities, C' and C, is equal to the difference between the two sums of money paid for them, M' and M. In other words the difference in value between the two sets of commodities is equal to the profit made in the first leg of this double circuit: or to look at it in a different way, $C' - C$ is the commodity form of merchant profit. Profit now assumes the form of a definite mass of commodities. But acts of exchange no matter how complex cannot actually produce commodities; they can only lead to a change in their ownership. In the circuit of merchant capital this change is effected through unequal exchange. But the commodities whose ownership is transferred in this way originate in the sphere of production as the product of labour.

To summarise: merchant capital in particular, and circulation capital in general, must engage in unequal exchange in order to acquire surplus value and profit, but this profit like that of all capital finds its real origin in the sphere of production as the unrewarded product of labour. Unequal exchange therefore does not invalidate the law of value, on the contrary it is the way in which the law of value works with respect to circulation capital.

2. *Circulation capital in capitalist society*

To illustrate how circulation and productive capital combine, consider the relatively simple situation where merchant capital buys the commodities of productive firms and sells them to their final consumers.

We start with the familiar circuit of industrial capital, $M - C_{MP}{}^L \ldots P \ldots C' - M'$ and extend its final phase to make the activities of merchant capital fully apparent. The sequence of events is exactly the same as those we have previously studied, only productive capital no longer sells the commodity it produces, C', to final consumers, but to a specialised form of retailers. The modified circuit which describes this process has the following form:

$$M - C_{MP}^L \ldots P \ldots C'$$
$$M^M \qquad M'$$

Here M^M represents the amount of money which merchant capital pays to productive capital for C', and the circuit of merchant capital is thus $M^M - C' - M'$. Maintaining the condition that capital as a whole engages in equivalent exchange, the value of M' and C' must be the same: i.e. capital sells the commodities it produces at prices equivalent to their value. Denied any profit from its sales merchant capital can only survive by purchasing commodities below their value: i.e. the value of M^M must be less than C'. This reconciles two apparently opposed conditions – capital as a whole trades at value while merchant capital engages in unequal exchange.

As no merchant will trade unless his buying price is less than his selling price, M' sets the upper limit to the value of M^M. Its lower limit is determined by the value of M, that is the value that productive capital advances at the beginning of the circuit. When productive capital sells its output, C', to merchant capital, the commodities being exchanged already contain surplus value, so that the relative values of M, M^M and M' determine the distribution of surplus value between the two forms of capital. Thus:

(1) If $M = M^M$, merchant capital appropriates all surplus value.

(2) If $M^M = M'$, productive capital is the sole beneficiary of exploitation.

(3) For both forms of capital to profit it is necessary for M^M to exceed M but fall short of M'.

The profits of the two forms of capital are thus inversely related – the greater the one the smaller the other. This rule applies to productive capital and circulation capital in all circumstances since social profit has a definite magnitude equal to the amount of surplus value produced by labour. It is important to see how this rule applies with respect to the other form of circulation capital, *finance capital*.

In addition to the marketing of the final products, the circulation of commodities requires complex financial arrangements, such as the provision of funds to productive capital at the start of the circuit, and the supply of consumer credit at its close. These are undertaken by specialist firms such as banks, merchant banks and building societies, who all have one thing in common; the only commodity they handle is money. This is the quintessence of the capitalist dream and apparently a complete escape from the law of value for profits are realised without the need to handle commodities let alone confront labour. Wealth that breeds wealth: money that makes money. It is an entertaining paradox that such a fantastic illusion arises from the activities of that fraction of the capitalist class most noted for its sobriety.

What happens in reality when a bank lends a manufacturer money? For the sake of simplicity, assume it lends him the full amount for both the constant and variable elements of capital. If this amount is represented as M^f, and the larger amount received back in return as M'^f, the circuit of finance capital is $M^f - M'^f$. This inserts into the circuit of industrial capital as follows:

$$M^f - M - C_{MP}^L \ldots P \ldots C' - M' - M'^f$$

As $M^f = M$, by assumption, for both forms of capital to profit (1) M'^f must exceed M^f – the profit of finance capital; and (2) this amount must be less than the difference between M' and M (i.e. $M' - M > M'^f - M^f$) – the profit productive capital.

Thus exactly the same conditions prevail here as above: the profits of finance capital are a deduction from the surplus value first appropriated by productive capital and then lost through unequal exchange. In the case of finance capital the inequality is blatant as one sum of money is exchanged for a greater sum.

At first sight productive capital and circulation capital appear antagonistic as they compete against each other for their profits. On the other hand, as their profits all come from the same source, they have a common interest that overrides their competition.

Although competition is only of secondary importance in capitalist society, this does not mean that it can be ignored. Competition between productive and circulation capital differs from competition among firms within each sphere in one important respect: whereas internal competition within a sphere can lead in principle to the destruction of all firms but one, competition between spheres cannot easily be pursued to this extreme. For a manufacturing company the rival is dispensable, but banks and retailers are vital. The production of cars, for example, could be undertaken by one firm; equally one bank or retailer could operate alone: but productive capital cannot operate without circulation capital and vice versa. For this reason concentration and centralisation has taken place mainly within rather than across spheres.

In practice the interdependence of productive capital and circulation capital is more important than their competition, but actually harder to discern and analyse.

Firstly productive capital is always the determining element in the partnership since production in general always takes precedence over circulation. The realisation of surplus value in the sphere of circulation is indispensable to capitalist production, but the exploitation of labour in the sphere of production is its premise. The relationship between productive capital and the working class is always decisive, but the framework within which it is organised is set by circulation capital particularly finance capital in its role as 'book-keeper'.[3]

In every form of society producers have to make some calculations about production: what is needed to attain a certain output; how much time is required and so on. Where

[3] See Marx, *Capital*, vol. 2, pp. 133–5.

production is organised on a small scale, these calculations are relatively simple: peasants, for example, do their sums in their head. As the scale of production grows and its social organisation becomes more complex, book-keeping also increases in size and complexity and demands the attentions of specialised workers. In capitalist society, all but the smallest firms employ such workers. Moreover, the role of this book-keeping tends to change as firms develop: in smaller firms it does little more than record performance, whereas in larger firms it plays a decisive role in planning future enterprises. It scarcely needs remarking that book-keeping is essentially a quantitative activity concerned exclusively with exchange value and profit. In its passive role it calculates how well firms have done in exploiting labour: in its active role it explores different avenues of exploitation and directs strategy. Each firm has its own book-keeping department: finance capital, the banks in particular, are the book-keepers of social capital. In their roles as lenders directing capital from one branch of production to another, and from firm to firm, they plan the exploitation of labour. Their situation at the beginning and end of the circuit of industrial capital gives them the power to execute this plan. Further, the very simplicity of their circuit, $M - M'$, keeps their attention firmly fixed on the real business of capital – the production of surplus value and profit. Their vision is not obscured by any of the considerations of technology and labour regulation which necessarily preoccupy the productive capitalists. As they always lend money to firms that make the highest rate of profit, for these loans are the most profitable, their sectional interests correspond perfectly with the general interests of capital. Removed from the actual arena of value of production they have become the main medium through which the law of value is communicated to all sectors of the capitalist economy.[4]

The role of merchant capital is essentially similar in that it favours those productive firms that are most efficient since these produce a larger amount of surplus value to be shared out. Historically, merchant capital preceded financial capital as

[4] Capitalism has created an accounting apparatus in the shape of banks ... Without big banks socialism would be impossible' (V. I. Lenin, *Can the Bolsheviks Retain State Power? Selected Works*, vol. 3, (London: Lawrence and Wishart, 1971), p. 376).

the main medium of the law of value, and, as we shall see, played a decisive role, in this respect, in the underdeveloped world. In the developed capitalist world there is no fundamental contradiction between circulation capital and productive capital. Individual producers who find their credit cut off or prices forced down against them by large retailers might think otherwise, but such inefficient firms are only sacrifices to the general interests of capital. In the last analysis there is always an identity of interest between capital in the sphere of circulation and capital in the sphere of production. Or to put in another way: in capitalist society no fundamental contradiction exists between the sphere of circulation and the sphere of production because both are under the control of the same class. In non-capitalist societies, however, where capital exists in the one sphere but not in the other, a contradiction does arise between the spheres and can develop into the decisive aspect of their history.

3. *Circulation capital in non-capitalist society*

For circulation capital to exist it is not necessary for the process of production itself to be organised upon a capitalist basis. The only conditions it requires are that part of the social product should regularly consist of commodities, i.e. goods for the express purpose of exchange, and money. The mode of production is immaterial; it can be organised by primitive communities or independent peasants; it can be based upon slavery, or be feudal in character. So long as there is an established market, capital can operate in the sphere of circulation.[5] In particular merchant capital can flourish, and it is a historical fact that this type of capital arose long before the industrial revolution in Britain saw the establishment of capitalist production proper – i.e. industrial capitalism. Merchant capital is,

[5] 'Within its process of circulation, in which merchant capital functions either as money or commodities (i.e. when it functions as merchant capital), the circuit of industrial capital . . . crosses the commodity circulation of the most diverse modes of social production, so far as they produce commodities. No matter whether commodities are the output of production based on slavery, of peasants . . . of state enterprise . . . on the basis of serfdom or of half-savage hunting tribes etc – as commodities and money they come face to face with the money and commodities in which industrial capital presents itself and enter . . . into its circuit . . .' (Marx, *Capital*, vol. 2, p. 110).

historically speaking, the oldest form of capital; the form in which it first appeared in the world. It existed in classical times in Greece and Rome and was present in Europe throughout the feudal epoch. It also flourished independently in many parts of the underdeveloped world long before they were 'discovered' by Europeans. Its modern history starts in the sixteenth century when it created the framework of the world market and laid the foundations of underdevelopment as well as development.

The general features of merchant capital are the same in every type of society in which it operates – capitalist or noncapitalist. It has no direct control over the labour process and is always dependent upon the class which does, even where it dominates this class. Secondly, it must always engage in unequal exchange to appropriate part of the surplus product of society. Thirdly, as capital it is always driven to accumulate and in this way acts as a medium through which the law of value is brought to bear on all parts of the economy, particularly the sphere of production. The repercussions of these features, however, do differ with the nature of society.

In non-capitalist society it has an independent class existence. It is the only form of capital and is penned up in the sphere of circulation while the process of production lies under the control of a non-capitalist class. In capitalist society the competition between the spheres of production and circulation is purely quantitative, involving the distribution of surplus value between the same class: in non-capitalist society it has a qualitative dimension. The accumulation of merchant capital requires an expansion of commodity production which sooner or later disrupts the social organisation of production itself. Even where merchant capital does not threaten to seize control of production directly and reorganise it on a capitalist basis – i.e. transform itself into industrial capital – by always challenging the social organisation of production it undermines the economic and social basis of the ruling class. As the sole form of capital and the sole medium of the law of value; which its drive to accumulate transmits all spheres of economic activity, merchant capital is the acid in which the structures of non-capitalist society are dissolved.

But all the time merchant capital menaces the position of the

dominant class in the sphere of production, it remains dependent upon it, for this is the class that organises the exploitation
of labour. As a result, its contribution to the general economic
development of society is always ambiguous and contradictory.

By encouraging commodity production which increases the
division of labour and stimulates productivity, merchant capital
not only plays a positive part in the development of the productive forces of society, it also opens the way for the reorganisation of production upon a capitalist basis. But historically
merchant capital has never been able to effect this transition
to capitalism proper itself.[6] Its dependence upon the non-
capitalist class that is directly responsible for their exploitation
of labour leads it to support this class at the very moment it is
undermining it. Its revolutionary edge is always blunted by
this conservative bias. This is fully apparent in the effects it has
on the development of production. On the one side there are
the positive effects we have just noted that arise from the stim-
ulus it gives to commodity production; on the other there are
negative effects since the surplus product that it appropriates
remains locked up in the sphere of circulation. Merchant
capital is trading capital and the surplus value it seizes is used
to expand trade not the forces of production. In fact it drains
part of the surplus product out of the sphere of production, and
the more it develops the more ennervating its effects. Thus
Marx concluded: 'The independent development of merchant
capital (i.e. as the sole form of capital) . . . stands in inverse
proportion to the general economic development of society'.[7]
The history of underdevelopment is the fullest expression we
have of these contradictory tendencies of merchant capital to
both stimulate and repress the development of the forces of
production and to both open and block the way for the full
development of capitalism.

[6] 'On the one hand, all development of merchant capital tends to give
production more and more the character of production for exchange value
and to turn products more and more into commodities. Yet its development
. . . is incapable by itself of promoting and explaining the transition from
one mode of production to another' (Marx, *Capital*, vol. 3, p. 327).

[7] Marx, *Capital*, vol. 3, p. 328.

5. Merchant Capital and Underdevelopment

Merchant capital discovered what subsequently became the underdeveloped world more than two and a half centuries before the first triumph of industrial capitalism in Britain at the end of the eighteenth century. The vast commercial empires set up first by the Spanish and Portuguese and later by the British, French and Dutch, established the basis of the modern economy. They concentrated vast accumulations of wealth in the form of capital, while overthrowing and pillaging whole civilisations. The creation of the world market, 'the starting point of the modern history of capital', was also a process of destruction. On the one hand it drew the world together into a new global division of labour that opened the possibility of previously undreamt-of increases in men's productive powers; on the other it split it apart, turning this division of labour into a grotesque structure of exploitation and oppression. The foundations of modern development and underdevelopment were laid at the same time by the same process.

Merchants do not make their profits by revolutionising production but by controlling markets, and the greater the control they are able to exercise the higher their rate of profit. For this reason merchant capital tends to centralise and concentrate itself into monopolies even faster than productive capital. For example, ten small merchants operating in a market will make less profit overall than a single company, as the competition among them weakens them *vis-à-vis* the producers and consumers at whose expense they prosper. Thus merchant capital in the days of its supremacy before the advent of industrial capitalism never embraced the advantages of competition but strived to form monopolies wherever it could, locally, in particular markets and internationally. It eschewed the principles of *laisser-faire* and sought state support for monopolistic privileges. As a result the contribution it made to the development of the forces of production was always ambiguous. Rising out of the pores of feudal society, it broke down the coherence of the old economic order subjecting production to the rationality of the market and acted as the medium through which the law of value first entered economic history. Yet it was constitutionally incapable of consummating the process that it set in motion. It could never overcome its specific nature of merchant capital and realise its general nature as capital; it could never break out of the sphere of circulation and impose the law of value directly on the sphere of production. It corroded the feudal order but in the last analysis was always dependent upon it. It was revolutionary and conservative at the same time. It opened the way for industrial capitalism but also blocked its progress. In eighteenth-century Britain it frustrated the rising class of industrial capitalists by denying them free access to markets and forcing them to operate within its own monopolistic market structures; it prevented free competition between the new and the old orders. It created the pre-conditions for a thorough-going revolution in the means of production, but its fractional interests, its desire to protect narrow monopolistic privileges, blocked their realisation. As a result the first struggle of industrial capitalism was against its own progenitor: the industrial revolution was a historic defeat for merchant capital. Its monopolistic privileges were attacked and destroyed by the new order whose call to battle was *laisser-faire*, free trade and competition.[1]

In the underdeveloped world, partly because of the manner in which the existing economic structures had been broken down by merchant capital in its era of supremacy before 1800, and partly because of the manner in which industrial capitalism triumphed in the developed countries, and turned the overseas empire of merchant capital to its own advantage, a similar

---

[1] Only in the sense of a struggle against an earlier mode of production, can competition be considered as an inherent property of capital. 'Free competition has dissolved the barriers of earlier relations and mode of production . . .' But the way it has been studied has led to the 'greater absurdity of regarding it as the collision of unfettered individuals who are determined by their own interests – as the mutual repulsion and attraction of free individuals, and hence as the absolute mode of existence of free individuality in the sphere of consumption and exchange. Nothing could be more mistaken' (Marx, *Grundrisse*, p. 649).

breakthrough proved impossible for almost one hundred and fifty years. And when it finally came after the Second World War it reinforced rather than undermined the structures of underdevelopment that had been established in the intervening period.

1. *The transition to industrial capitalism*

At first sight economic conditions in the underdeveloped world at the end of the Second World War bear a close resemblance to those in many developed countries on the eve of their industrialisation. At one level there are the superficial similarities of original underdevelopment – poverty, low productivity, the heavy dependence upon agricultural production and so on. More fundamentally is the importance of merchant capital which in both sets of countries had stimulated commodity production and undermined the coherence of the existing pre-capitalist modes. Furthermore, in the underdeveloped countries this century, just as in the developed countries in the past, merchant capital has remained dependent upon these non-capitalist structures, so that its revolutionary role has been countered by conservative tendency to protect the status quo. But these similarities are overwhelmed by two major differences.

First, merchant capital in the underdeveloped world does not have local roots but originated from the developed countries. The underdeveloped countries were drawn into the world market in a way quite different from that of the developed countries. They were the colonised not the colonisers, and of all the many consequences of this fact one stands out. Where the destructive depradations of merchant capital were controlled in their homelands by the state and the powerful social classes represented within it, there was no force to withstand it overseas. Wherever it went sooner or later it broke down all opposition and pursued its interests in a completely unrestrained fashion. Whereas in Britain, for example, merchant capital could only operate within definite political limits which recognised other social interests; in India, to take an important example from the underdeveloped world, no such limits existed. For a period the East India Company abrogated political power to itself and acted as the state. The result was not the relatively slow transformation of the economic structure on the basis of which a revolutionary reconstruction of the social and political order could eventually take place; but a sharp rupture in the process of historical development. In the Americas and Australia whole civilisations were wiped out; West Africa was reduced to a slave market and no society escaped without being turned into a corrupt parody of its former self. The degree of social incoherence that arose would have made the establishment of industrial capitalism impossible even if this had been historically practical. What it did allow, in fact what it made essential, was external colonial domination, either direct or indirect, and in this way it gave a spurious basis to the hypocritical claims of the colonising powers that they brought civilisation and order to a world of barbarism and chaos.

The second difference arises from the changes that overcame merchant capital as a result of industrialisation. We have seen that merchant capital has two historical forms: in non-capitalist societies it exists as the sole, and in this sense, independent form of capital; whereas in capitalist society it exists only as an aspect of industrial capital, a form which the latter must assume, or a necessary moment, in its circuit. Before the nineteenth century merchant capital existed solely in the first of these forms throughout the whole world, though, as we have just seen, its historical significance varied according to whether it was of domestic or foreign origin. The industrial revolution marked a watershed in its history, for the triumph of industrial capitalism changed it from its first to its second form. The change was not, of course, immediate, but was drawn out over several decades. Furthermore, it was a change that merchant capital resisted as it engaged in a massive defensive struggle on many fronts of which the most significant, certainly for our purposes, concerned the role of the state, particularly with respect to tariffs. In Britain, merchant capital as an independent form of capital, retained its power for almost a hundred years after the rise of industrial capital in the middle of the eighteenth century, until it was fatally undermined by the parliamentary reforms of the 1830s and finally smashed by the Repeal of the Corn Laws in the 1840s. In the underdeveloped world it retained its independence much longer, but weakened in its home bases it could not totally withstand the force of industrial capital abroad.

The transformation of merchant capital in the underdeveloped world was decisively influenced by its own history in these areas and the effect it has upon them. We have seen that the disruption it caused here created a measure of social and political incoherence which made the establishment of industrial capitalism impossible. But, in fact, industrial capital had no such programme and saw the underdeveloped world as a market not as a sphere of direct investment and accumulation. So partly out of necessity but mainly because it concerns lay in a different direction, industrial capital took the underdeveloped world very much as it found it, leaving it as a final preserve for merchant capital. But if merchant capital retained its independence in the underdeveloped world, it was no longer allowed to trade solely on its own account but was forced to become the agent of industrial capital. In other words merchant capital in the underdeveloped world both retained and lost its independence. It remained the only form of capital present: but within the world economy as a whole it became an aspect of industrial capital. In other words, merchant capital in the underdeveloped countries after the establishment of industrial capitalism in the developed countries in the nineteenth century existed in its two historical forms simultaneously. At one and the same moment it was the only form of capital but not the only form of capital. This apparent paradox is the *specifica differentia* of underdevelopment, and its emergence as a historical fact in the course of the nineteenth century marks the beginning of underdevelopment as we know it.

We have seen, to use Marx's words, that 'the independent development of merchant capital … stands in inverse proportion to the general economic development of society'. In the context of the underdeveloped world we must add to this general tendency of merchant capital to depress the advance of production, its specific tendency to retard progress that arose from its role as the agent of industrial capital. More as the form of existence of industrial capital in the underdeveloped world, it was concerned not only with trade in general as a means of exploiting the producers but with the actual content of the trade, with the use-values that were exchanged. All forms of capital are primarily concerned with the quantitative aspects of commodities, with their value expressed as exchange value, but productive capital which is directly concerned with material production is forced to pay close attention to their qualitative aspect, that is to their use-value. In its independent form where it is separated from the spheres of production and consumption and has no direct responsibility for them, merchant capital trades where it can and what it can without concern or scruple: here slaves; there opium. But industrial capital is directly involved in the process of social reproduction, and so must pay closer attention to its requirements than merchant capital. It is forced to be more *civilised*. And merchant capital in so far as it acts as its agent is forced to adopt a similar code and drop many of its bad habits.

What were the interests of industrial capital in the under-developed world; interests which merchant capital, as its agent, was obliged to pursue? First, it saw the underdeveloped world as an indispensable source of necessary means of production, particularly raw materials of which cotton was by far and away the most important throughout much of the nineteenth century. Later, as industrial production progressed in the developed countries other commodities like rubber, tin, bauxite, copper and so on became prominent. Not only were these materials indispensable to the productive process, but acquired cheaply they offered a direct means of maintaining the rate of profit and offsetting any tendency for it to fall. Its second interest, to acquire a reliable and cheap supply of means of consumption, such as, first, wheat, and later other forms of food, was moti-vated by the same concern over the rate of profit. For the lower the value of food, the lower is the value of labour-power and therefore the social wage, and the greater the amount of profit. Third, the underdeveloped world presented industrial capital with a vast potential market in which it could not only realise the surplus value extracted from the proletariat in the developed world, but could augment it with the surplus product of the non-capitalist world appropriated through unequal exchange, i.e. by selling commodities in the markets of the underdeveloped world at prices that exceeded their values. Its profits were equally enhanced by unequal exchange in the other direction, that is by buying raw materials and food below their values.

Merchant capital with its long experience of this type of business was ideally suited to act as its agent, which is the first reason for its retaining such a substantial degree of independence in this area for so long.

The second reason is that the reorganisation of production in the underdeveloped world that this pattern of trade required did not need substantial capitalisation, and the direct involvement of productive capital, on a massive scale. The manner in which export production was organised varied from one underdeveloped country to the next, partly in response to the social conditions that prevailed, and partly by the nature of the commodity produced and exported. In some countries production remained in the hands of peasants who either undertook it willingly or a result of political compulsion of one form or another. In other countries exporting agricultural commodities, production was undertaken by expatriate controlled plantations which appear at first sight to be a form of fully developed capitalist production. In those countries which exported minerals we again encounter what appears to be capitalist production. For both mines and plantations employed wage-labour, and in many cases the firms involved were subsidiaries of productive firms in the developed countries. In some ways it would be wrong not to recognise these undertakings as capitalist, for they possess all its formal qualities. On the other hand they have certain features which suggest that it would not be completely correct to treat them in this way. Firstly, they invariably relied upon migrant labour which stayed for only a relatively short time, and until the end of the Second World War they never set about creating a permanent labour force. This was not an accidental development but shows every sign of being part of a carefully conceived strategy of low wages. Their second peculiarity is essentially a different expression of this strategy; namely, the very low degree of capitalisation. The main element of production was living labour, the vast bulk of which was illiterate and unskilled, working with the assistance of very few instruments. It can, of course, be claimed that neither of these features change the fundamental character of these enterprises as capitalist but merely define them as a particular type of capitalist enterprise. Whatever one decides on this question the broad issue seems unchanged; that the reorganisation of production in the underdeveloped countries which industrial capital required, needed only a minimum involvement on its part so that the major responsibility for this task could be, and was, in fact, carried out by merchant capital.

We have already touched upon the third reason why merchant capital survived so long in the underdeveloped countries as an independent form of capital. Even if industrial capital had wished to migrate to the underdeveloped world on any substantial scale, it would have found the environment unwelcoming because of the degree of social disruption brought about during the first phase of mercantile development. In fact, the conditions which merchant capital had created throughout the underdeveloped world by the middle of the nineteenth century were absolutely unconducive to the full development of capitalism. But there is yet a further reason for its staying on the sidelines the importance of which is easy to underestimate: we have seen that the triumph of industrial capitalism involved a long struggle against merchant capital. By the middle of the nineteenth century industrial capital had won decisive victories in the metropoles but merchant capital remained powerful in the overseas empires. The result was an uneasy stalemate in which merchant capital was both winner and loser. It both lost and retained its independence and subsequently existed simultaneously in its two historical forms. The consequences were doubly depressing for the underdeveloped world: on the one side the tendency of merchant capital to repress general economic development in proportion to its own independent development; on the other the reorganisation of whole economies to the requirements of external economic interests.

In recent years this twofold consequence of merchant capital for the economies of the underdeveloped world, corresponding to its own twofold nature as independent merchant capital and the agent of industrial capital, has been characterised by radical development economists as the economics of *dependence*. But this concept fails to grasp the real nature of the process of underdevelopment. The immediate explanation for this is the theoretical framework employed. This does not recognise the law of value but is an electric combination of orthodox economic theory and revolutionary phraseology, seasoned with supposedly self-explanatory facts, such as data concerning the pattern of trade and capital movements, and spiced with cynical quotations by Western politicians and businessmen on their aims and the methods adopted to achieve them. The conclusions reached are not wrong in so far as they go, only they cannot get beyond the level of general ideological critique. Turning their backs on the law of value the best they could achieve was a historical account of the process of underdevelopment elaborated through empirical categories, such as *dependence, metropole* and *satellite*, which collapse into hopeless contradiction in the face of close investigation. For example, if underdevelopment is the result of dependence, that is the subordination of one economy to another, then certainly Canada, with over half its manufacturing industry owned by American firms and its agricultural sector dependent upon the world market over which it has no control, must be considered underdeveloped; and to less extent, perhaps, many Western European countries whose most important branches of industrial production – electronics, petrochemicals and cars – are often dominated by the same American firms, must fall into the same category. In other words, the concepts of development and underdevelopment, as used by radical development economists, have not overcome the relative nature which orthodox neo-classical theory bestowed upon. They have not become distinct, though inseparable concepts, and therefore do not correspond in a scientifically adequate way to the actual processes of development and underdevelopment which are themselves distinct but nevertheless inseparable as aspects of the general process of capitalist development.

On the other hand these economists have made an important discovery. In contradistinction to the classical Marxist view that capital breaks down all non-capitalist modes of production and creates 'a world after its own image', i.e. a developed world; they have shown that capital, despite its corrosive effects, has bolstered up archaic political and economic forms through a series of alliances with powerful elements in the pre-capitalist orders. But they have not discovered why this is the case: because capital in these countries existed in the form of independent merchant capital. Or to go a step further, in the underdeveloped world independent merchant capital was the form of existence of industrial capital. And that the behaviour of capital here – now revolutionary in establishing commodity production, now reactionary in supporting the existing non-capitalist order – is typical of capital when it exists in this form.[2]

2. *British colonialism*

The history of underdevelopment proper, as opposed to its pre-history, opened in the middle of the nineteenth century when industrial capital completed the subordination of merchant capital in Britain. At this time Britain was not only the leading industrial country but also the major imperial power with colonies and spheres of influence in North and South America, the Mediterranean and South East Europe, Africa and Asia. Developments in Britain therefore had powerful repercussions throughout the whole world: in fact, for more than fifty years following 1850, they were the decisive factor in world economic history. The most important political medium through which they were transmitted overseas was direct colonial control, and its practice of *indirect rule* was the clear political counterpart of capital as it existed in the underdeveloped world. For this form of political administration reproduced at the level of the state all the ambiguities that merchant capital created in the economic sphere. It established a centralised political authority upholding private property and money, but rested its power, in part at least, on local groups whose own power originated in non-capitalist forms of society.

The starting point of modern British colonialism was the reorganisation of the colonial state in India following the Mutiny in 1857. The India Act of 1859 and the Declaration substantially reduced the direct political power of the East India Company and recognised Indian religious rights and

[2] Many of the shortcomings of radical theory arise from the manner in which it criticised orthodox dualism. So keen were the radicals to show that capitalism was responsible for underdevelopment, that in arguing that the whole underdeveloped world was caught up in the world capitalist economy they claimed that production in the underdeveloped world was everywhere capitalist production. In doing so they confused commodity production with capitalist production. Gunder Frank, in particular, was guilty of this error. See Ernesto Laclau, 'Imperialism in Latin America', *New Left Review*, No. 67 (May–June 1971).

political institutions only to use them as instruments of control. Here the pattern was set for the modern colonial empire. Behind the hypocritical claim that the best way to bring civilisation to the world was to allow *native* institutions to survive and then try to turn them in a more enlightened direction by exposing them to British influence, lay a number of harsh realities. Above all, there was the need to establish an administrative and material infrastructure for the regular and reliable trade that industrial capital demanded. This required the establishment of political control over huge and widely dispersed populations, but as the resources and manpower at the disposal of the various colonial governments were strictly limited, some form of local buttressing was necessary. Moreover, given the size of the British Empire in relation to Britain itself, it is obvious that this could never have been achieved without a significant amount of local support. It is true that at any one point in its empire the British could bring vastly superior force to bear than any opposition, but this was not the case overall. Moreover, as the British were generally unprepared to spend large amounts from the imperial exchequer in policing their empire, but sought to make all the colonies self-sufficient in the area of law and order, indirect rule, the devolution of power, was as much a matter of necessity as free choice.

The outcome was a curious paradox: the establishment of a series of capitalist states with deep roots in non-capitalist societies which they were forced to protect as the foundation of their power. But at the same time they also represented a social force that systematically undermined these societies. For the existence of merchant capital – and to exist it had to accumulate – led inevitably to the spread of commodity production. As a result, colonial policy was full of all sorts of ambiguities. At one moment it encouraged capital but at the same time the colonial authorities were always reluctant to allow large-scale investment in their territories; and during the twentieth century, British capital, when its attitude to the underdeveloped world began to change, experienced considerable frustration on this score. Certainly the bulk of British capital invested abroad, even before the First World War, did not find its way into British territories. In short, in the British colonies, we have the political counterpart of merchant capital – states that on the one hand opened the way for capital but on the other tried to restrain its accumulation.

There is one further point we must take up at this stage: the explicit commitment of the British colonial authorities to *laisser-faire*, which has led some writers to characterise British imperialism as free trade imperialism. At first sight this appears inconsistent with the important role played by merchant capital in the British colonial empire since we remarked earlier free trade is no part of its style or credo. But, in the first place, the colonial commitment to free trade was more apparent than real. What it meant in practice was not free trade between the colonies and the rest of the world as much as free trade between British capital in the colonies and capital in Britain. It was a policy aimed to serve narrow sectional interests dressed up in general terms. Moreover, whenever free trade threatened British interests as happened on occasions when a group of colonial producers were able to compete effectively with British enterprise, allegiance to the holy grail was either forgotten or carefully avoided.[3] In the second place, it must be remembered that merchant capital in the colonies was also the representative of industrial capital and this is the real reason for its series of *volte-faces* on this question. Free trade and competition were necessary for industrial capital to break down the non-capitalist modes of production which existed throughout the colonial world and force them into a subordinate trading relation. In fact, the extent to which merchant capital in the British colonial empire embraced an ideological position totally alien to its very nature and one which had been previously used so effectively against it, is the clearest possible indication of the extent to which it had become transformed by the triumph of industrial capitalism. In the era of capitalist production proper it acquired a wholly new significance, as indeed did trade in general.

3. *The theory of unequal exchange*

The importance of trade as a mechanism of the exploitation of the underdeveloped world plays a central part in the one recent theory of underdevelopment which seeks to base itself fully on

[3] See G. B. Kay, *The Political Economy of Colonialism in Ghana* (London: Cambridge University Press, 1972).

the law of value. This is Arghiri Emmanuel's work on unequal exchange.[4] Although his theory is a travesty, its recognition of the law of value raises a number of important issues that are relevant to the question in hand.

Emmanuel's thesis that the underdeveloped countries are exploited through unequal exchange, that is by selling their commodities below value and buying others above value, is, with one vitally important qualification which we shall make in a moment, undoubtedly true. This is because a great many of the economic ties between the developed and underdeveloped countries, more in the past than today, are mediated through merchant capital. Emmanuel offers a different explanation for this, which is not only invalid in its method but is based upon a number of unacceptable premises leading to the absurd conclusion that the workers of the developed countries benefit from the exploitation of the peoples of the underdeveloped world to an extent that rules out any possibility of an alliance among them against capital – '. . . the antagonism between rich and poor countries is likely to prevail over that between classes'.[5]

As we have just mentioned Emmanuel does not explain unequal exchange in terms of the operations of merchant capital; he sees it quite differently as a result of the way in which values are transformed into prices. In order to understand his work we must therefore briefly summarise the *transformation problem* which is one of the most complex and controversial parts of Marx's economic theory.[6]

Let us start by assuming a fully developed capitalist society in which there are two branches of industry, one that produces means of consumption and the other means of production. In the first instance, we assume that the ratios of values employed

---

[4] Arghini Emmanuel, *Unequal Exchange*.

[5] Ibid., p. 176 et seq.

[6] 'There has been a great deal of confusion about the so-called problem of the "transformation of values into prices", but, once it is freed from its metaphysical associations, it turns out to be merely an analytical puzzle which, like all puzzles, ceases to be of interest once it has been solved' (Joan Robinson and John Eatwell, *An Introduction to Modern Economics*, p. 30). For a concise statement of the problem see Paul M. Sweezy, *The Theory of Capitalist Development*, Monthly Review, Modern Reader Paperback Edition (New York and London, 1968), chap. VII.

and produced in the two industries are identical. As the issue is not affected one way or the other by the absolute magnitudes involved, we will simplify one step further and assume initially that the two branches of industry are exactly the same size. The situation can be depicted as follows:

TABLE 1

Branch	Constant capital	Variable capital	Surplus value	Value of output	Organic composition of capital	Rate of surplus value	Rate of profit
	c	v	s	$o=c+v+s$	c/v	s/v	$p=\dfrac{s}{c+v}$
I	80	20	20	120	4	100%	20%
II	80	20	20	120	4	100%	20%

But what happens if conditions within the separate branches of industry should vary?

TABLE 2

Branch	Constant capital	Variable capital	Surplus value	Value of output	Organic composition of capital	Rate of surplus value	Rate of profit
	c	v	s	$o=c+v+s$	c/v	s/v	$p=\dfrac{s}{c+v}$
I	80	20	20	120	4	100%	20%
II	60	40	40	140	1·5	100%	40%

The first branch of industry has remained the same but the second has changed. The total capital advanced has remained constant ($c + v = 100$) and the rate of surplus value is still equal to 100 per cent, but two important changes have taken place. First the organic composition of capital in branch two has fallen from 4 to 1·5, and secondly, the rate of profit has risen from 20 per cent to 40 per cent. The second change is consequent upon the first. Other things being equal, particularly the rate of surplus value, the rate of profit will move in an opposite direction to the organic composition of capital. From this it follows: if there are two industries in an economy each of which has the same rate of surplus value but different organic compositions of capital, and furthermore, if both these industries sell their output at its value, the capitalists in the two industries will achieve different rates of profit. This rule is general in that it applies to any number of industrial branches.

We now come to the crux of the problem. For obvious reasons, Marx claimed, there must be a *general rate of profit* ruling in the economy; that is to say, there must be an equal rate of profit in all branches of industry. If this were not the case capital would inevitably flow to that branch where the rate of profit was highest, in our example branch two, which would mean an excessive production of means of production. But without an adequate supply of consumer goods the workers could not maintain themselves and production as a whole would soon grind to a standstill. In other words, the need for a general rate of profit arises from the law of social reproduction itself. But if different branches of industry have different organic compositions of capital – and technical reasons alone ensure that this must be the case – the existence of this general rate of profit is inconsistent with equivalent exchange. If two branches did sell their commodities at equivalent prices, the branch with the lower organic composition of capital would show a higher rate of profit than that with the higher organic composition. Moreover, if this happened, capital would have no incentive to increase the organic composition of capital and improve methods of production. Thus the equivalent exchange of commodities is not only inconsistent with the general rate of profit, it is also inconsistent with the most essential features of capitalist development. Many economists have considered this inconsistency so fundamental and irresolvable as to invalidate the law of value entirely. However, it can be resolved in a way perfectly consistent with the law of value.

The first feature of the solution must be that individual commodities do *not* exchange at prices equivalent to their values: there must be unequal exchange. But as Marx never claimed that the prices of individual commodities were equal to their values, this is no concession whatsoever. The law of value states that the prices of all commodities taken together must be equivalent to their collective value, and that the prices of individual commodities are not necessarily equal to their values but are determined by them; which is something quite different from a simple theory of equal exchange. Thus the most fundamental statement of the law of value already indicates the solution to this problem: commodities produced in branches of industry with a lower than average organic composition of capital sell below their values to compensate for the excessive profit that would accrue to capital here if they sold at value; while commodities produced in industries with a higher than average organic composition of capital sell above value for the same reason; subject to the overriding and definitional constraint that the two total prices paid for all commodities are exactly equal to their values. In general terms this is the transformation problem and its solution.

To understand it in more detail we must introduce two new concepts. The first is the *cost price* of a commodity: this is not the value of the commodity but the value that has to be advanced for its production. Thus

$$\text{value} \qquad c + v + s$$
$$\text{cost price} = c + v$$

so that difference between the two is surplus value. If we represent the cost price as q, the rate of profit is $\frac{s}{q}$. The second new concept, the *price of production*, the price at which commodities are actually sold, is more complex as it embodies the whole solution in itself.

Table 3 is essentially the same as table 2, but it incorporates these two new concepts and adds a final row which deals with social capital. The column relating to the rate of profit now covers the general rate of profit. This is calculated by dividing the total constant and variable capital advanced into the total surplus value that is produced. To get the price of production we merely inflate the cost price by this value: here equal to 30 per cent. Thus as both branches of industry in our example, have the same cost price, equal to 100, both have the same price of production, 130. In other words, both branches of industry sell their commodities at the same price: but while they fetch the same price on market, they have different values. Exchange is unequal. Branch 1 sells commodities with a value of 120 for a price of 130; while branch 2 gets only the same price for commodities worth 140. But although the value and prices of individual commodities are not equal, total value and total prices are the same at 160. If we substitute 'developed countries'

TABLE 3

Branch	Constant capital	Variable capital	Surplus value	Value	Organic composition of capital	Rate of surplus value	Cost price	General rate of profit	Price of production
	c	v	s	$o=c+v+s$	c/v	s/v	$q=c+v$	P'	$c+v+p'=q+p'$
I	80	20	20	120	4	100%	100		130
II	60	40	40	140	1·5	100%	100	30%	130
Social capital	140	60	60	260	2·3	100%	200		260

for branch 1 and 'underdeveloped countries' for branch 2
– a measure upon whose legitimacy we will comment in a
moment – we have the essence of Emmanuel's theory. The
developed countries sell commodities to the underdeveloped
countries at prices that exceed their values and buy from them
commodities at prices below values, so that every transaction
between the two sets of countries involves a drain of value out
of the underdeveloped countries and thus reduces the pace of
accumulation there.

But this is only half the story: Emmanuel calls it unequal
exchange in the 'narrow sense'. There is also what he calls
unequal exchange in the 'broad sense'.

Leaving aside for the moment the factors that may have first
brought it about, let us assume that the value of wages goes
up by 50 per cent in the developed countries – i.e. variable
capital rises from 20 to 30 – and surplus value falls correspondingly – from 20 to 10 – with everything else remaining constant.
Table 4 depicts this new situation and the effects it has upon the
rate of profit and the prices of production. Firstly, although it
has no immediate impact on branch II, the underdeveloped
countries, it brings down the general rate of surplus value, from
100 to 70·1 per cent, and the general rate of profit, from 30 to
26·3 per cent. Secondly, although the value of production is
unaltered throughout, the prices of production are changed in
a way that is even more favourable to the developed countries.
In fact, the 'terms of trade' move against the underdeveloped
countries by 9·1 per cent.[7] Here, Emmanuel claims, is decisive
proof that the improved living standards of the working class
in the developed countries are paid for, in part at least, by the
underdeveloped countries.

[7] This figure is arrived at as follows: first four ratios are calculated

(1) The ratio of prices of production to value for developed countries
   in table 3:

$$\frac{130}{120} = 108·3$$

(2) The ratio of prices of production to value for underdeveloped countries in table 3:

$$\frac{130}{140} = 92·8$$

TABLE 4

Branch	Constant capital	Variable capital	Surplus value	Value	Organic composition of capital	Rate of surplus value	Cost price	General rate of profit	Price of production
	c	v	s	$o=c+v+s$	c/v	s/v	$q=c+v$	P'	$c+v+P'=q+p'$
I	80	30	10	120	2·6	33%	110		136·2
II	60	40	40	140	1·5	100%	100	26·3%	123·6
Social capital	140	70	50	260	2	70·1%	210		260

Emmanuel, however, cannot rest his case here, for at this stage the increase in wages is hanging in the air as an arbitrary assumption. If it is left like this, there is no reason to suppose that workers in the underdeveloped countries could not redress the situation by increasing their wages by a similar amount or by even more. As it happens, Emmanuel does not attempt to deal with this question theoretically, but relies upon what he considers the indisputable and unambiguous fact that wages have gone up in the developed countries while remaining low throughout the underdeveloped world. But as we saw in Chapter 3 the increase in wages is far more ambiguous than it appears at first sight. The size of the wage can be measured in two ways: either in terms of its value or the mass of commodities it can purchase. If the value of commodities remains constant no problems arise on this score and an increase in one measure will lead to an exactly corresponding increase in the other. But if the value of commodities falls, real wages can increase without the value of the wage going up at all: in fact, if the value of commodities falls sufficiently real wages can rise while the value of wages actually drops. Emmanuel makes no distinction between these two measurements of the wage, and his assumption that the rise in wages in the developed countries is

---

(3) The ratio of prices of production to value for developed countries in table 4:

$$\frac{136 \cdot 2}{120} = 113 \cdot 5$$

(4) The ratio of prices of production to value for underdeveloped countries in table 4:

$$\frac{123 \cdot 6}{140} = 88 \cdot 3$$

Next calculate (2) as a ratio of (1) $\quad \dfrac{92 \cdot 8}{108 \cdot 3} = 85 \cdot 6$

and (3) as a ratio of (1) $\quad \dfrac{88 \cdot 3}{113 \cdot 5} = 77 \cdot 8$

Finally express the second of these ratios as a percentage of the first:

$$\frac{77 \cdot 8}{85 \cdot 6} = 90 \cdot 9\%$$

or a reduction in exchange ratios of the underdeveloped countries of $9 \cdot 1\%$.

an unambiguous fact that can be taken as given is totally insub-
stantial. Certainly there is no disputing that real wages have
risen considerably in the developed countries and that they are
generally much higher than wages in the underdeveloped
countries: on the other hand labour productivity is higher in
the developed countries and the value of commodities correspondingly lower. In terms of value it is more than likely that
wages in the developed countries are lower than those in the
underdeveloped countries.

Although this seriously undermines Emmanuel's argument
it does not totally invalidate it, for he can always claim that
wages in the developed countries are nevertheless higher as a
result of the exploitation of the underdeveloped world than
they would otherwise be. But this assumes that the advantages
gained from unequal exchange accrue to labour and not
capital: workers are able to buy imported goods at prices below
their value. But capital is unlikely to stand idly by in this
circumstance and see the fruits of its imperial efforts accrue to
its class enemy at home. Undoubtedly it is happy to see the
price of imported consumer goods come down; part of its
imperial programme was directed to this end. But the aim of
the exercise was not to increase the living standards of the working class, but by reducing the prices of their means of necessary
consumption to reduce the value of wages. Whether any reduction on this score equals or falls short of the gains from unequal
exchange – whether, that is, the gains accrue to capital or
labour, and in what proportions – is impossible to say. The
degree of uncertainty surrounding this matter makes it a
fragile foundation for the major political thesis that Emmanuel
erects upon it. Certainly, if wages are equal to the value of
labour-power, unequal exchange in the realm of international
trade cannot affect them at all. Where this condition holds all
it can to do is transfer surplus value from capital in the underdeveloped countries to capital in the developed countries. This
is not unimportant and it can be put forward as a factor
slowing down accumulation in the underdeveloped world. But
it lends no support whatsoever to Emmanuel's central thesis
that the working class of the developed countries benefit from
exploitation in the underdeveloped world.

We must now consider the legitimacy of Emmanuel's method

of analysis. Can the use of transformation analysis be justified in this context? Can a method of analysis designed to deal with the relationships between different branches of industry within a fully developed capitalist economy be applied to the trade relationships between countries, particularly when production in one set of countries is not organised on a totally capitalist basis?

There are two ways of approaching the capitalist world economy. One stresses the primary importance of class relationships and makes relations between nations – i.e. international relations – firmly dependent upon them. The other adopts the completely opposite position of making the nation state its primary unit. The class struggle between labour and capital in any one country is overshadowed by the shared national interests of the two classes. This, of course, is a most simple statement of a highly complex issue which requires the closest theoretical and historical analysis. Emmanuel's way of coping with it is to adopt a method which already has one approach built into it from the start and then claim that his analysis has proved the correctness of that approach. The approach he favours is, of course, the second: 'the antagonism between rich and poor countries is likely to prevail over that between classes'. His method, the substitution of countries for branches in the schemes of transformation, already embodies this position, for it necessarily lays a primary stress upon international relations and makes the class struggle a secondary factor. The idea of unequal exchange that he subsequently derives, thus already embodies this position: it does not prove it for the simple reason that no analysis can prove the validity of a position that is already built into it. Nor can the particular conclusions derived about the inequality of exchange – conclusions which are dubious even in their own terms – be cited as evidence of their significance. Emmanuel does not show that unequal exchange between developed and underdeveloped countries makes international antagonisms more important than class antagonisms; rather he uses the assertion that this is the case as the basis for a particular theory of unequal exchange.[8]

[8] Moreover, the redistribution of surplus value between different capital that takes place through the transformation of values into prices does not prove the existence of deep antagonisms between the branches of capital involved. On the contrary, capitalist competition is the moment in which

Moreover his theory is fundamentally ahistorical. He takes the nation states of the underdeveloped countries as a datum assuming on the one hand that they have the same historical significance as those of the developed countries, and on the other, that they represent the interests of every class of society there, at least, in so far as they stand in opposition to the developed countries. But it is manifestly apparent in the case of those underdeveloped countries which were colonies – it is less clear but not less true for those that were never the victims of direct colonisation – that the *independent* nation states they now possess were largely created by capitalist interests from the developed countries. Without pursuing the question too far, it is perfectly clear that their history is quite different from that of the developed countries, and that to treat them as identical, as Emmanuel does, is a formalistic absurdity. Or to put the matter in a different way: the very existence of the underdeveloped countries is already evidence of class forces having shaped the world and its political institutions into a mould that reflected their logic. To analyse these forms independently of the class relationships that have created them is like, for instance, attempting to understand traffic laws without reference to the car. And to continue this analogy further: it is true that all vehicles are now subject to traffic laws, but to claim that these laws are independent of the development of road transport, that it is they which have determined the pattern of this development, would be manifestly absurd. Yet this is exactly the type of thing Emmanuel is suggesting about the relationship between nation states and underdevelopment.

According to Emmanuel the exploitation of producers in the underdeveloped world has two moments. Firstly they are exploited by their own capitalists, and secondly, through the mechanisms of unequal exchange, by the capitalists of the

---

individual capitalists become conscious of their collective interests. In fact Emmanuel's analysis can be turned on its head, for it can be shown that unequal exchange notwithstanding, the higher the rate of surplus value in the developed world, other things being equal the higher the rate of profit in the underdeveloped countries. And from this it follows that capital throughout the whole world has a common interest against those whom it exploits irrespective of their nationality. Or what is to say the same thing, the exploited peoples of the world have a common class enemy – capital.

developed world. But where foreign capital is directly invested
in the export industries of the underdeveloped countries these
two moments are fused into one; the exploitation of workers
in situ involves in itself an international transfer of value from
the nationals of one country to those of another. Moreover, this
transfer is effected without the need for unequal exchange in
international trade. Emmanuel's theory is only applicable to
situations where export production in the underdeveloped
world is organised by national capital; but this has happened
far less often than Emmanuel necessarily assumes. Even where
it does operate, unequal exchange has far more limited effects
than Emmanuel supposes. Within the rules of transformation
analysis unequal exchange affects the distribution of surplus
value – i.e. it affects the relationship between different capitals,
but not between capital and labour. Operating internationally,
unequal exchange can lead to a redistribution of surplus value
to the benefit of metropolitan capital and the detriment of
national capital from the underdeveloped world, but it has no
direct effect one way or another on the rate of exploitation in
either developed or underdeveloped countries.

Where export production in the underdeveloped world is
organised on a non-capitalist basis the use of transformation
analysis which assumes fully developed capitalist production is
totally unjustifiable. Paradoxically, however, it is in just this
situation that unequal exchange does affect the rate of exploitation. For, here, the capital of the developed countries is
represented by merchant capital and unequal exchange is an
essential part of its way of doing business.

4. *Merchant capital and the development of underdevelopment*

We must now return to the main theme of this chapter, the role
of merchant capital as the agent of industrial capital in shaping
underdevelopment. In this role merchant capital from the
developed countries purchases raw materials, for example, from
their non-capitalist producers in the underdeveloped world and
sells them to productive capital in Britain. These are then used
to produce manufactured commodities some of which merchant
capital purchases for sale back to the underdeveloped countries.
In this type of trade, therefore, merchant capital undertakes
four acts of exchange, two of buying and two of selling, so that

its circuit has the following form:

$$M - c - M' - C - M''$$

(1) $M - c$, at beginning of the circuit, is the purchase of raw materials in the underdeveloped countries.

(2) $c - M'$ is the sale of these materials to productive capital in the developed world.

(3) $M' - C$, merchant capital buys some of the output of productive capital; and

(4) $C' - M''$ completes its circuit by selling it in the underdeveloped world.

As we take a closer look at this circuit we see that profits in the first half, equal to $M' - M$, can be derived from two sources. First, the merchant can buy raw materials in the underdeveloped world below their value (i.e. the value of M is less than that of c) and sell them above value to productive capital in the developed world (i.e. the value of M' exceeds that of c). The profit on the first transaction is a direct deduction of surplus from the producers of the raw materials; that on the second an indirect confiscation of surplus value from productive capital. For if a capitalist who engages in production is forced to pay a price for his means of production that exceeds their value, he is in effect forfeiting some of his surplus value before he actually gets hold of it. A similar situation exists in the second part of the circuit, $M' - C - M''$, where profits are equal to $M'' - M'$. Here the profits of the merchant capitalist will be greater the lower the price at which he buys from productive capital: this part of profit constitutes a direct deduction from the surplus value of productive capital. Equally his profits will benefit according to the price he charges his customers in the underdeveloped world: if he charges a price that exceeds the value of the commodities he sells, this is an indirect form of exploitation – indirect since it is exploitation that takes place in the sphere of consumption rather than production. Thus merchant capital has two sources of profits: the surplus value of productive capital in the developed countries and the surplus product of non-capitalist producers in the underdeveloped world.

In principle, as the following numerical example shows, merchant capital can derive profit equally from these two sources.

$$1000\ M - 1100\ c - 1200\ M' - 1300\ C - 1400\ M''$$

Its total profit here, £100, is acquired equally from all four of its transactions.

(1) 1000 M – 1100 c: the merchant in the underdeveloped world buys raw materials worth £1100 for only £1000;

(2) 1100 c – 1200 M: he sells them to a British capitalist for £100 more than they are worth for £1200;

(3) 1200 M – 1300 C: he now buys for £1200 manufactured commodities worth £1300;

(4) 1300 C' – 1400 M'': these commodities are now sold for £100 more than their value in the underdeveloped world.

In each transaction the merchant makes a profit of £100, but since two of the transactions take place in the underdeveloped world (i.e. M – c and C' – M') and two in the developed world (i.e. c – M' and M' – C) both sets of countries contribute equally to his profit.

In practice, however, there is no reason for this to happen, and in fact, it rarely does. The following example shows how the same total profit can be derived entirely from one source, the underdeveloped world:

$$1000\ M - 1200\ c \quad 1200\ M' - 1200\ C - 1400\ M''$$

Here the merchant acquires profit from only the first and last transactions; that is, from the purchase of raw materials and the sale of manufactured commodities in the underdeveloped world. His second and third transactions, those with productive capital in the developed world, take place at value and yield him no profit whatsoever. In this case his profits come entirely out of the surplus produced in the underdeveloped world and he is unable to get hold of any of the surplus value of productive capital in the developed countries.

A third possibility, where values of the following order prevail, must be considered in detail.

$$1000\ M - 1200\ c - 1100\ M' - 1000\ C - 1200\ M''$$

(1) 1000 M – 1200 c: the merchant buys raw materials worth £1200 for only £1000;

(2) 1200 c – 1100 M': he sells the raw materials to productive capitalists in the developed world apparently making a loss of £100. But as he only paid £1000 for them in the first place he has in fact made a profit of £100 (1100M' – 1000 M).

(3) 1100 M' – 1000 C: the merchant now buys manufactured commodities worth £1000 for £1100 thus wiping out the profit he has made so far; but

(4) 1000 C – 1200 M, he more than compensates for this by selling them in the underdeveloped world for £1200.

In one important respect this example is identical to the one that preceded it: in both the loss to the people of the underdeveloped world is £400. They lose £200 at the beginning of the circuit when they sell raw materials worth £1200 for only £1000; and £200 at the end when they buy manufactured goods worth £1000 for £1200. But in this case the profit of merchant capital amounts to only £200 (i.e. 1200 M'' – 1000 M), the other £200 is appropriated by productive capital, whose overall profits are correspondingly that much greater. Now, productive capital in the developed countries begins to benefit directly from exploitation in the underdeveloped world. But these are made at expense of merchant capital which can, as the following example shows, lose all its profits in this way.

$$1000 \ M - 1200 \ c - 1000 \ M' - 800 \ C - 1000 \ M''$$

(1) The merchant buys for £1000 raw materials worth £1200, so at this stage he is £200 up;

(2) 1200 c – 1000 M': as he can only sell them for £1000 his profits are wiped out;

(3) 1000 M' – 800 C: he now makes a further loss by purchasing manufactured commodities for £200 above their value;

(4) 800 C – 1000 M'': he makes good this loss by selling these commodities for £200 above their value in the underdeveloped world.

Here again the people of the underdeveloped world have made a loss of £400, and again through unequal exchange with merchant capital which has bought their exports for £200 less than they are worth and sold them imports for £200 more; but merchant capital itself makes no profit. It starts with £1000 and finishes with the same amount: all the profit in this case goes to productive capital. Of course this is a limiting case, and no merchant firm would advance capital in a trade that brought in no profit at all. In fact merchant capital would withdraw from this business before profits when they dropped belo~~w~~ age rate of profit in its home country. What usuall~~y~~ when productive capital draws the profits out of th~~e~~ merchant capital, is that the merchant firms los~~e~~ withdraw their capital, and allow their trading interests in the underdeveloped world to be nationalised with favourable terms of compensation.

History cannot be invented as a series of simple schemata such as these; on the other hand there is no doubt they do represent in a rudimentary form real changes that have taken place. As industrial capital developed in Britain, and other countries in the nineteenth century, the role of merchant capital was transformed. Not only did it lose its independence at home but its imperial role was now subordinated to the new force. As this happened its ability to profit from the home leg of overseas trade declined, and it had to rely increasingly on the surplus it could extract abroad. But even these profits were not sacrosanct and productive capital began to eat into them. All merchant capital could do was to try to increase its profits abroad through ever-more unequal exchange: an initiative experienced in the underdeveloped world as a decline in its terms of trade. But the possibilities for merchant capital to increase the rate of exploitation are severely limited. In the last analysis the rate of exploitation in any society depends upon the productivity of labour, which industrial capital continuously strives to increase by revolutionising the methods of production. But merchant capital, locked up in the sphere of circulation, has no power in these areas. Plantation production and mines run with cheap labour bear few resemblances to modern industrial production, and certainly offered merchant capital no way out in the long run. In fact the situation of merchant capital was doubly jeopardised; for not only did it find itself losing profits to industrial capital as its prospects of increasing exploitation in the underdeveloped world ran out; but as capital it was driven by its very nature to accumulate and this meant not merely maintaining profits but actually increasing them. By the beginning of the twentieth century merchant capital was already facing a crisis in many parts of the world in which its particular form of merchant capital was negating its general character as capital.

The crisis of merchant capital can be posed in different terms. We have seen that after the triumph of industrial capitalism in the developed countries, merchant capital existed in the underdeveloped world simultaneously in its two historical forms; as independent merchant capital trading on its own behalf, and as the agent of industrial capital. On the one hand it tried to secure profits for itself, on the other profits for industrial capital. So long as the rate of exploitation in the underdeveloped world increased, and the profits at the disposal of merchant capital went up, the contradiction between these two forms could be held in check. But as the rate of exploitation ceased to grow merchant capital faced a crisis. Initially it sponsored an increase in productivity by encouraging commodity production, and with it an extension of the division of labour; but subsequently it was unable from its situation in the sphere of circulation to increase it any further. As its profits dwindled merchant capital began to lose the last remnants of independence and was forced to act simply as the agent of industrial capital. But even here it ceased to serve either its own interests or those of industrial capital. To survive as capital it was forced out of trade directly into the sphere of production; that is, it was forced to act as productive capital openly. At the same time productive capital which had previously restricted its activities to the developed world, finding its rate of profit from the underdeveloped countries ceasing to grow if not actually decline, was obliged to intervene directly. The result was a new phase in the history of underdevelopment: the inception of a capitalist mode of production proper in the underdeveloped world. But capital could not wipe out its own history and begin as though nothing had happened previously: it was forced to operate in the conditions of underdevelopment which it had itself created: conditions that were quite different from those that prevailed in the developed countries in the eighteenth and nineteenth centuries. Thus when industrialisation finally started in the underdeveloped world in the 1930s and picked up steam in the post-war period, it was a process altogether different from that which had taken place earlier in the developed countries. It took place in conditions of deeply established underdevelopment which it could not overcome but only reinforce.

6. Industrial Capital and Underdevelopment

The collapse of primary commodity prices during the depression of the 1930s brought all the pressures bearing on merchant capital to a head. The savagely reduced prices it was forced to pay producers in a desperate attempt to protect its profits carried the crisis into the underdeveloped world, which responded with nationalist opposition to the whole political and economic order established in the nineteenth century. This marked the beginning of the end for the phase of underdevelopment in which merchant capital had mediated between the capitalist and non-capitalist worlds and productive capital had scarcely strayed from its homelands.

The transition from this phase to the new one, whose distinguishing feature was the establishment of industrial production in the underdeveloped world, covered many years and proceeded much more rapidly in some countries than others. As a global process, it began between the world wars, although in some parts of Africa, for example, it did not start until the late fifties: in many parts of that continent it is even now barely under way. Moreover, it must be remembered, this new phase does not involve a total transformation in the economic structure of the underdeveloped countries. They remain dependent upon the export of primary commodities, non-capitalist production persists and merchant capital continues in its quasi-independent form. But for all this the establishment of productive capital and the beginnings of industrial capitalism represents a decisive moment in the history of underdevelopment. Today, it is quite wrong to think of the underdeveloped countries simply as centres of primary production, primary producers and exporters; for industrial production both in a material and a social sense, is now one of the essential features of their economies. In fact, industrialisation is now such an integral part of underdevelopment that it can no longer be considered as its solution, at least not in its present capitalist form.

Those countries in which the process of industrialisation got under way most quickly, were, first of all, those in which primary production for export was most advanced, and the depression of the thirties was experienced not as a temporary hiatus but as a sign that a particular phase of productive development was drawing to a close. Secondly, there were the countries in which primary production was organised in such a way that net revenue already took the form of capital, or could easily become capital. Thirdly, they were countries whose political constitution conceded sufficient power to local interests to allow them to pressure the state into constructing tariff walls to protect their new industrial ventures from outside competition. In Brazil, for example, all these conditions were present, and the period of world economic depression before the Second World War was one of rapid industrial expansion.[1] Furthermore this expansion was the result of local enterprise and capital. After the war matters changed in this respect when foreign capital from the developed countries, particularly the United States, intervened directly and took a controlling interest. This intervention was not of course limited to Brazil, but occurred throughout the whole of the underdeveloped world; as Western capital, recovering first from the depression and then from the war, reorganised its global diminance. As the establishment and growth of industrial capitalism in the underdeveloped countries took place within the context of world wide decolonisation and the growth of national independence, it was widely and willingly mistaken as the beginnings of economic development.

This process of industrialisation, however, differed not only in its historical context from that which had taken place earlier in the developed countries, it was also, and largely as a result of this difference, structurally quite dissimilar. It was *partial*: not just in the sense of being restricted to certain branches of industry – the processing of primary commodities for export, and import substitution of consumer goods – but in that it only offered employment to a limited section of the proletariat.

[1] See Celso Furtudo, *Diagnosis of the Brazilian Crisis* (Berkeley and Los Angeles: University of California Press, 1966).

At first the unemployment that accompanied industrialisation appeared a simple consequence of its late start and slow progress; and, as such, a problem that would be resolved in time if only growth could be accelerated. But by the mid-sixties it was quite clear that unemployment was a permanent feature of the scene. 'In the first half of the 1960's', write Baer and Hervé, 'a note of concern, often bordering on disillusionment, could be observed among the most ardent industrialisation advocates. The dynamic sector of the economy (i.e. productive capital) was not absorbing labour at a satisfactory rate.'[2] The immediate source of this concern was a United Nations Report, *The Growth of World Industry, 1938–1961*,[3] whose statistical findings Baer and Hervé summarised carefully. Table 1, which presents a condensed version of their work, shows that in all the countries covered industrial output rose much more rapidly than employment.

TABLE 1

Growth of Manufacturing Industry and Employment in
Selected Countries Annual Growth Rates: 1950–1960

	Output	Employment
Argentina	4·4	2·0
Brazil	9·8	2·6
Chile	5·4	1·7
Peru	6·6	4·4
Colombia	7·6	2·5
Venezuela	13·0	2·1
Mexico	6·5	0·4
India	6·8	3·3
Egypt	5·5	3·9

In fact as the authors point out, the growth of industrial employment failed to keep up with the growth of urban population. In Latin America during the years 1945–60, urban population grew at 4·3 per cent per annum; the growth of the economically active population in the non-agricultural sector

[2] W. Baer and M. E. Hervé, 'Employment and Industrialisation in Developing Countries', in ed. by Richard Jolly, Emmanuel de Kadt, Hans Singer and Fiona Wilson, *Third World Employment* (London: Penguin Books, 1973), p. 269.
[3] *The Growth of World Industry, 1938–1961* (New York: United Nations, 1965).

was 3·9 per cent but industrial employment went up only 2·8 per cent. According to Sutcliffe, who has examined statistics produced by the International Labour Office, a similar story can be told for Africa and Asia.[4] In short, by the mid-sixties the *employment gap* had become visible even to the statisticians.

Furthermore, all the evidence suggests that this gap cannot be attributed to the slow expansion of industry. In Brazil, for example, which achieved one of the highest rates of industrial expansion in Latin America, industrial employment grew at

TABLE 2

Number of Unemployed in Certain Countries of Africa and Asia
1953–1967 (in thousands)

	1953	1958	1967
Africa:			
Cameroon	0·2	1·3	1·6
Chad	—	0·1	0·2
Ghana	6·0	9·0	17·0
Madagascar	—	0·6	0·7
Morocco	—	35·0	24·0
Nigeria	—	5·0	20·0
Sierra Leone	1·6	2·6	9·0
Upper Volta	—	0·2	0·4
Zambia	—	3·0	12·0
Asia:			
Ceylon	55·0	115·0	250·0
Cyprus	2·7	2·5	2·9
India	480·0	1050·0	2710·0
Iraq	—	1·2	3·7
Malaysia	—	20·0	105·0
Pakistan	9·5	140·0	180·0
Philippines	—	760·0	960·0
South Korea	—	350·0	590·0

only 2·6 per cent per annum during the fifties, while urban population expanded more than twice as fast at 5·4 per cent. Much the same is happening in Africa where it appears that unemployment is growing most rapidly in those countries with the highest rate of industrial expansion.[5] And the problem gets

[4] R. B. Sutcliffe, *Industry and Underdevelopment* (London and Massachu-setts: Addison-Wesley Publishing Company, 1971), p. 120.

[5] 'This phenomenon (i.e. unemployment) has been noted in economies such as Puerto Rico and India with high population densities as well as in the relatively underpopulated countries of Africa. Those countries which are industrialising rapidly seem to suffer from this phenomenon just as

worse rather than better. A study of the Zambian copper industry concluded that 'if the same ratio of African labour to copper output prevailed in 1959 as in 1949, African employment in the industry would have been 69,000 instead of 35,000.'[6]

The immediate cause of the problem is easy enough to identify, namely the widespread adoption of so-called capital-intensive techniques; methods of production, that is, which employed relatively few workers in relation to constant capital. The most obvious explanation for this, and one widely favoured by structuralists, is that underdeveloped countries who do not produce their own equipment have to import it from the developed world.[7] There, it is claimed, because of the relative scarcity of

---

much, if not more, than those which are not industrialising quickly' (C. R. Frenk, 'Urban Unemployment and Economic Growth in Africa', in ed. Jolly, de Kadt, Singer and Wilson, *Third World Unemployment*, p. 302.

[6] Cited by H. Myint, *The Economics of Developing Countries*, p. 65.

[7] Other explanations have been advanced. Baer and Hervé look for the causes in terms of a scarcity of skilled labour. Unskilled labour, they argue, must be employed alongside skilled labour so that the number of skilled workers will act as a constraint upon overall employment. In the underdeveloped countries it comes into play before the capital constraint, so given the number of workers who can work on the one hand and the amount of capital available on the other, we can deduce the overall capital-output ratio. But the argument is based upon arbitrary assumptions. First, the ratio of skilled to unskilled workers is assumed independent of the choice of technique. Secondly, it is assumed fixed while the capital-output ratio is assumed variable, although no reasons for this are advanced. Thirdly, the shortage of skilled labour, which is essentially a short-term phenomenon, or at worst a medium-term problem, is used to explain a long-term development. Baer and Hervé, in *Third World Employment*, p. 280. Other economists have argued that factor prices in the underdeveloped countries do not reflect factor efficiencies: the international mobility of capital makes its price too low, while trade unions force wages up too high. Whenever a neo-classical economist believes factor prices are out of line, it is always due to wages being too high! The inadequacy of this approach is its absurd assumption that relative factor prices should reflect relative efficiencies and that international capital mobility and trade unionism are somehow anomalous features of capitalist development. In neo-classical economics when a discrepancy arises between theory and the reality it seeks to explain, it is always the reality that is wrong. See Myint, *The Economics of Developing Countries*, p. 65 et seq. and Charles P. Kirdleberger, *Economic Development*, 2nd ed. (New York and London: McGraw-Hill, 1965), p. 255.

labour the only equipment produced for home needs and export embodies highly mechanised techniques. In other words, the adoption of methods of production not suited to their local requirements is imposed on the underdeveloped world.[8] We shall see that the theoretical premises on which this analysis is based are fundamentally false. But there are even more immediate reasons for doubting it. If firms in the underdeveloped world really wanted relatively simple equipment to make full use of the plentiful supplies of labour around them, in the way that structuralist (i.e. neo-classical) economists suggest they should, it would surely be profitable for capital in the developed countries to produce it. But the evidence suggests that no such demand exists, for where firms do have a choice they generally favour techniques which involve higher degrees of mechanisation. Thus the only conclusion we can reasonably draw is that these methods are the most efficient from the point of view of capital, even where labour is plentiful and their adoption results in the growth of widespread unemployment. In other words the situation in many underdeveloped countries where industrial output speeds ahead with a growing section of the population left in dire need and poverty is one more expression of the absurdity of accumulation as a principle of social organisation.

1. *Fixed and circulating capital*

What then determines the choice of technique and the pattern of technical development in capitalist society? To understand the concepts necessary to deal with this question we must go back over some ground already covered, and look again at the process of capitalist production.

---

[8] 'Technology is not disembodied but is embodied in certain capital goods. In a sense therefore technology has always been the basis of metropolitan monopoly. The underdeveloped areas have been unable to establish a complete industrial structure because they have been unable to establish the industries possessing at the time the most complex and advanced technology. In that case the basis of monopoly has shifted not to a new category, technology, but to a new more restricted group of capital goods industries' (Sutcliffe, in ed. Owen and Sutcliffe, *Studies in the Theory of Imperialism*, p. 190). Even Marxists seem unable to avoid commodity fetishism and understand that the relation between things is a fantastic mystification of the relations between men.

Let us return to the example of car production discussed in Chapter 2. It will be recalled that the 10,000 cars produced each year had a total value of £6 mn, half of which was new value created by living labour, and half of which arose from the constant capital productively consumed by his labour. This constant capital was made up of £2 mn of machinery and other instruments of production, and £1 mn of materials. Variable capital equalled £1·5 mn and as the rate of exploitation was 100 per cent, surplus value also equalled £1·5 mn. Thus:

$$2 \text{ mn } c + 1 \text{ mn } c' + 1·5 \text{ mn } v + 1·5 \text{ mn } s = 6 \text{ mn } o = 10,000 \text{ cars}$$

when all the symbols have the same meaning, only c now refers to that part of constant capital made up of machinery and instruments of labour, while c' represents the other part of constant capital, the materials of labour.

In this context, it is clear that both c and c' refer to the value of the two types of constant capital consumed in the production of the 10,000 cars, which, we have assumed, takes one year. Now consider what happens during the first year. The firm advances £1·5 mn as variable capital and no more, since capitalists only pay workers after they have worked and are not in the habit of paying them in advance. Further, it is reasonable to assume that it buys only those materials of labour needed for current production, and does not carry large stocks, so that the amount advanced as constant capital under this head, c', will not exceed the £1 mn that is used. But we cannot reasonably make the same assumption about the other part of constant capital, c, the instruments of labour because of the technical conditions of production particularly in modern manufacturing industry. At the start of production capitalists have to set up their whole plant whose value is far in excess of what c represents here, and whose lifetime far exceeds a single year. In other words, capital has to advance far more on this part of constant capital than is needed for a single year's production. In material terms: this capital remains intact after the first year; depending upon its durability and a number of other factors, it might still be intact after five years. From the point of view of the initial outlay, however, the lifetime of these machines does not matter, since they have to be bought *in toto* before a firm can go into business.

To the various distinctions in the types and form of capital already made, we must now add another: that between *fixed* and *circulating* capital. If for the moment we take one year as a basic unit of time, we can distinguish between these two types of productive capital provisionally in the following terms: fixed capital is that part of productive capital whose lifetime exceeds one year in the sense that it does not yield up its total value in this time but nevertheless has to be paid for in full at the start of production; while circulating capital comprises those items which are fully consumed in the course of one year and are paid for currently one year at a time.

To illustrate this distinction, we can again use the example of car production and assume all the relationships are the same but production requires the installation of a plant that has an active lifetime of *six* years and is capable of producing 60,000 cars. Thus six years' production can be described as follows:

$$12 \text{ mn } K + 6 \text{ mn } C' + 9 \text{ mn } V + 9 \text{ mn } S = 36 \text{ mn } O = 60{,}000 \text{ cars}$$

where K represents fixed capital or that part of constant capital which is installed at the start of production and survives the whole period. All the fundamental relations of production are the same in this six-year schema as they were in that of one year's production: in particular, the rate of surplus value is the same in both instances.

At this stage we must introduce the concept of the *turnover* of capital. We have seen that the characteristic feature of all capital is movement, in the sense of a continuous change in form. Moreover, as this movement is always systematic bringing capital back to the particular form in which it started, it can be conceived as a circuit. The most basic circuit of capital is $M - C - M'$ as this expresses unambiguously its inherent drive to accumulate. The movement of capital from the first pole of the circuit to the last, here from money to money, $M \rightarrow M$, is called its turnover, and the time it takes to complete a circuit is called the *period of turnover*.

The concept of the circuit and therefore those of turnover and period of turnover, apply not only to the broad historical forms of capital – merchant capital $(M - C - M')$ and industrial capital $(M - C_{MP}^L \ldots P \ldots C' \ldots M')$ – but to the specific forms that capital assumes within them. Thus, within the framework of industrial capital, there is the circuit of productive capital:

$$P \ldots C' - M' - C_{MP}^L \ldots P$$

Starting with capital in its productive form, P, we move to the commodities that are produced, C', which are sold, M', whereupon the money-capital is reinvested and the circuit is complete as we arrive back with productive capital, $C_{MP}^L \ldots P$. The movement from $P \ldots P$ is the turnover of productive capital and the time it takes is its period of turnover.

Now we can define the distinction between fixed and circulating capital more precisely. Although the movement $P \ldots P$ defines the turnover of productive capital in general, different elements of productive capital circulate at different rates. The whole of its variable element and that part of constant capital which comprises the materials of labour turns over much more rapidly than the constant capital that is made up of instruments of labour. That is to say, its *whole* value is embodied in produced commodities, C', converted money, M' and returned to its original form of productive capital. But only a fraction of the value of the instruments of labour equal to c, passes into product and then into money where it remains temporarily immobilised. For example, at the end of one year's production, the car firm will have recovered only £2 mn of its £12 mn outlay on plant and equipment, i.e. £2 mn c, which is too small to throw back into production. At the same time, it will have recovered the whole value of the capital advanced on materials of labour (1 mn c') and all its variable capital (1·5 mn v) which can be put back into production and complete their circuit. This part of productive capital which is able to complete a turnover in one year is called circulation capital; the other part whose turnover takes much longer is called fixed capital. It can be seen immediately the categories fixed and circulating capital are *not* the same as those of constant and variable capital. Some constant capital is fixed and some is circulating. Moreover, the categories of fixed and circulating capital do not supersede those of constant and variable capital in the analysis of capitalist production in general. While it is true that one part of constant capital always stands alongside variable capital under the head of circulating capital; when we consider the fundamental nature of capitalist production variable capital stands alone, and the labour-power it purchases remains the sole source of new value and surplus value.

According to its conventional definition as the ratio of constant to variable capital, the organic composition of capital[9] in car production is equal to 2, whether we calculate on the basis of six years' production (12 mn K + 6 mn C': 9 mn V) or one year's (2 mn c + 1 mn c': 1·5 mn v). But for reasons that should now be coming clear this ratio is a totally inadequate indicator of the degree of mechanisation of production, and therefore a poor guide to the effects of accumulation on employment. When we calculate the organic composition of capital on the basis of six years' production, we ignore the fact that variable capital has turned over six times during this period while the greater part of constant capital has turned over only once. When we calculate it on the basis of a single year's production we make an equally important omission: we take account of only that part of constant capital that yields up its value in this time and ignore the rest which although it is not productively consumed from the point of view of value has to be physically present for production to take place at all.

Let us look at the matter for the moment from the capitalist's point of view. To go into business he has first of all to set up *all* his machinery and equipment (fixed capital), which on our present assumptions involved him in an outlay of £12 mn. Secondly, he must keep by him enough money capital to secure the materials of labour he needs and pay the workers themselves. For the six years of the assumed lifetime of his plant this will require advances of £15 mn but he does not have to lay this amount out all at once, or even have it by. For we have

---

⁹ The composition of capital has two aspects: (1) the value-composition which is the ratio of the value of constant capital to that of variable capital; and (2) its material composition which is not directly quantifiable but relates to the way in which capital is divided into means of production and living labour-power as it functions in the process of production. 'Between the two there is a strict correlation. To express this, I call the value-composition of capital, in so far as it is determined by its technical composition and mirrors the changes of the latter, the *organic composition of capital*' (Marx, *Capital*, vol. 1, p. 625). The correlation between the two aspects of the composition of capital thus depends upon the movement of the values of labour-power and constant capital. In what follows we assume that these values remain constant in relation to each other.

assumed here, that circulating capital turns over in one year, i.e. the circuit $P'\dots C' - M' - C_{MP}{}^L\dots P'$, in which P' represents circulating capital, takes only one year to complete. From his point of view, this means that sales at the end of the first year yield sufficient revenue to buy materials and pay the workers during the following year, without any need on his part to dig into depreciation or similar funds (equal to the value of constant capital consumed, (c) or touch profits (s). Therefore he needs funds to cover only one year's value of circulating capital which comes to £2·5 mn as opposed to the six-year total of £15 mn. When this is added to the amount advanced as fixed capital we get a total investment of £14·5 mn of which only £1·5 mn takes the form of variable capital. The ratio of constant to variable capital calculated this way is 13 : 1·5 or 8·6 which is far in excess of the organic composition of capital equal to 2.

It must be emphasised that what is being pursued here is an indicator of the degree to which production is mechanised, and not an exact measure of mechanisation which is inconceivable anyway. What we are after is a guide to the effects of accumulation on employment and there is no doubt that the ratio we have just worked out, $(K + c')/v$ is much better in this respect than the conventional organic composition of capital, c/v, although later we shall modify it to make it even more appropriate. For this new ratio recognises that while all the constant capital is not actually consumed in the process of production in any given period such a year, it has to be all physically present all the time. Or to put it another way, while all the machinery that is consumed during the lifetime of a plant is involved in production all the time, only a fraction of the labour-power that is used up during the total life of the plant is actually employed at any one moment. Furthermore, this ratio gives a much more accurate indication of variable capital as a proportion of total capital advanced than the organic composition of capital.[10]

We can call this new ratio the organic composition of capital in the process of production, or, more simply, the *organic composition of production*, as it indicates the ratio in which constant and variable capital are actually present in the process of

[10] Marx makes this distinction between capital *consumed* and capital *employed* in *Capital*, vol. 1, p. 620.

production. In contradistinction to this, the conventional concept of the organic composition of capital indicates the ratio in which the two forms of productive capital enter the commodity, and we shall refer to it from now on as the organic composition of capital in the commodity, or, for short, the *organic composition of the commodity*. It is patently clear, as we have just seen, that the two ratios can have a different value: in our example, the organic composition of production is much higher than the organic composition of the commodity. They will only be the same when constant and variable capital turn over at the same rate: it is only because these turnover rates differ that they diverge at all. If we represent the period of turnover as t measured in years, so that t^v is the period of turnover of variable capital,[11] t^c the turnover period of that part of constant capital consisting of instruments of production, this can be quickly demonstrated.

$$\text{As } K = \frac{t^c}{t^v} c$$

the organic composition of production

$$= \frac{K + c'}{v}$$

$$= \frac{\dfrac{t^c}{t^v} c + c'}{v}$$

and the organic composition of the commodity

$$= \frac{c + c'}{v}$$

The only difference between the two is that t^c/t^v features in the numerator of the organic composition of production. But if

[11] Throughout the whole of this chapter we assume that the part of constant capital that purchases the materials of labour turns over at the same rate as variable capital, the other part of circulating capital. This might not be strictly true in practice, but it does not effect the analysis, and the assumption is therefore worth making on the grounds of simplification. What is true is that capital will do everything it can to reduce the turnover period of this constant capital and equate it to that of variable capital – by methods of 'scientific' stock control whose aim is to reduce the amount of necessary stocks.

$t^v = t^c$, this would be equal to 1 and the two ratios would be identical. Such an eventuality is not only remote but one which capital will avoid wherever it can. For other things being equal the greater the ratio $t^c : t^v$, i.e. the more rapid is the turnover of variable capital in relation to that of fixed constant capital, the higher is the rate of profit.

2. *The effect of turnover on the rate of profit*[12]

Where all the capital turns over at the same rate, the rate of profit is calculated as follows:

$$p' = \frac{s}{c + c' + v}$$

This was the formula used in Chapter 2 before the possibility of different rates of turnover was considered. In car production:

$$p' = \frac{1 \cdot 5 \text{ mn s}}{2 \text{ mn } c + 1 \text{ mn } c' + 1 \cdot 5 \text{ mn } v}$$

$$= 33 \cdot 3\%$$

But where the different parts of productive capital turn over at different rates it needs to be modified:

$$p' = \frac{s}{K + c' + v}$$

---

[12] Marx himself never explored the effects of turnover on the rate of profit in detail and it is interesting to note that chapter IV of *Capital*, vol. 3, entitled 'The effect of the turnover on the rate of profit', was added by Engels. The crucial passage, pp. 227–9, is also Engels' work. This does not mean that it is wrong, for it would be absurd to criticise Engels for not knowing Marx's theory. The problem seems to be a different one. Engels was working with an already structured text which was nevertheless incomplete and the many additions that he did realise needed making, had to be inserted into the existing structure. One can only surmise that if Marx had lived longer, he would have dealt with the effects of turnover on the rate of profit in very great detail, for all the elements of such a treatment are contained in the minute examination of turnover that exists in *Capital*, vol. 2. If this work had been carried out it is possible that volume 3, particularly the sections on the law of the falling tendency of the rate of profit, would have been different in many important respects and that these differences would have prevented many subsequent misunderstandings, as well as cutting off many criticisms before they could have been made.

In the revised example where it was assumed car production required £12 mn of fixed capital, the rate of profit is only 10·4 per cent.

$$p' = \frac{1·5 \text{ mn } s}{12 \text{ mn } K + 1 \text{ mn } c + 1·5 \text{ mn } v}$$

$$= 10·4\%$$

The differences between these two formulae is that the first takes account of only that part of constant capital whose value is actually transferred to the commodity, c, while the second considers the total amount of constant capital actually involved in production, K. The reason for this difference is straight-forward. The rate of profit measures the rate of possible accumulation, the rate, that is, at which a firm can expand. Consider the production of cars where an investment of £12 mn is required for fixed capital. To start production the firm has to lay out this amount in full, and in addition have sufficient finance to buy its necessary materials £1 mn, and pay its workers, £1·5 mn. It therefore needs £14·5 mn to commence operations. But at the end of first year's business it has only acquired £1·5 mn surplus value which can be used for further investment, so the rate at which it can expand is equal to £1·5 mn: £14·5 mn or 10·4 per cent – the rate of profit calculated by the second method.[13]

Clearly it would be best for capital if it could manage without any fixed capital at all, but as this is impossible it has to find other ways to increase its rate of profit. One is to increase

[13] If the technique of production is such that expansion cannot be made in a piecemeal fashion then the firm will have to wait 10 years before it can double its production. If, however, there are 10 firms in the economy, all the same, their combined surplus value will allow one of them to double production each year. But the rate of expansion of social capital will still be equal to 10% which is the general rate of profit. In order for firms to pool their surplus value in this way and make accumulation continuous and therefore faster, a system of credit is necessary. '. . . it is clear that . . . a pro-portional expansion of the whole business . . . is possible only within certain more or less narrow limits and, besides, requires such a volume of additional capital as can be supplied only by several years' accumulation of surplus value . . . But simultaneously with the development of capitalist production the credit system also develops. The money-capital which the capitalist cannot yet employ in his own business is employed by others who pay him interest for its use' (Marx, *Capital*, vol. 2, p. 321).

relative turnover, $t^o : t^v$, for this will lead to a rise in the rate of profit even if the rate of surplus value remains the same. To illustrate this, contrast our example of car production with another undertaking, say shipbuilding, which employs exactly the same amount of capital for the same period of time, exploits its workers at the same rate and turns out a commodity with the same organic composition of capital, Thus:

$$12 \text{ mn } K + 6 \text{ mn } c' + 9 \text{ mn } v + 9 \text{ mn } s = 36 \text{ mn } O = 36 \text{ mn } O'$$

where 36 mn O = 60,000 cars, and 36 mn O' is one ship. Assuming it takes six years to produce this output, a single year's output is as follows:

$$2 \text{ mn } c + 1 \text{ mn } c' + 1 \cdot 5 \text{ mn } v + 1 \cdot 5 \text{ mn } s = 6 \text{ mn } o = 6 \text{ mn } o'$$

where 6 mn o = 10,000 cars, and 6 mn o' = one-sixth of a ship. But this difference in use-value has a vital effect upon the rate of profit and therefore the rate of accumulation. Where the output of the car firm at the end of one year's production can be sold and the value it contains can be realised, this is not true of the output of the shipbuilding firm. On our assumptions it takes six years to build a single ship, which cannot be sold until it is finally complete. Thus although the value of the construction work done in a single year is exactly the same as that embodied in 10,000 cars, this value cannot be realised until the very end of the productive process. Quite simply the shipbuilder cannot sell his ship one-sixth at a time, and this determines the amount of capital he is forced to advance.

When the car firm sells 10,000 cars for £6 mn at the end of each year's production, it realises £2 mn of its fixed capital, £1 mn of it is constant circulating capital, £1·5 mn of his variable circulating capital, and £1·5 mn of surplus value. The first and last of these items, the value of fixed capital and surplus value realised, are of no immediate or direct use to it, as they are too small to be put back into the productive process.[14] But the amounts realised against the circulating part of capital can

---

[14] The surplus value will enter the credit system from where it will pass to another branch of production in which it can function as capital. The same will happen to the money realised against constant capital if it is not needed to maintain the plant and keep it in repair.

be used to finance the next year's operations. Thus, although in the course of six years' production £15 mn of circulating capital are *employed*, (6 mn C' +9 mn V) only £2·5 mn needs to be *advanced*. Because its circulating capital turns over in one year, the car firm need never have more than one year of it in hand: although it employs £15 mn of circulating capital during the six year life of its fixed capital, it never advances more than £2·5 mn. It makes up the £15 mn by advancing £2·5 mn six times. In the shipbuilding industry matters are quite different.

It is true that at the end of the first year the value of £2·5 mn circulating capital has passed into the product: i.e. 'circulating' capital has completed the first leg of its circuit $(P...C')$. But because one-sixth of a ship cannot be sold, this is as far as it can get. Until the ship is finally disposed of, which can only happen after six years, it remains stuck here, so to speak, unable to complete its circuit: $(C' - M' - C_{MP}{}^{L}...P)$. As it cannot be used by the firm to cover the costs of circulating capital for the following year new capital has to be advanced. In fact, as the firm cannot realise any capital at all until the end, it has to advance all the circulating capital it employs, i.e. the full £15 mn.

The differences between these two enterprises all pivot on the distinction between *capital employed* in production and *capital advanced*. As regards the former, capital employed, the two are identical: in six years both employ a capital value of £27 mn; i.e. 12 mn K + 6 mn C' + 9 mn V. But the value of capital advanced differs: the car firm advances £14·5 mn, £12 mn fixed and £2·5 mn circulating capital) while the shipbuilder advances £27 mn (£12 mn fixed and £15 mn circulating capital). As the rate of profit is calculated as the ratio of surplus value to total capital *advanced*, these two firms, identical in every respect but the value of capital advanced, must earn different rates of profit.

Although the shipbuilder employs the same amount of capital as the car manufacturer, he has to advance much more, £27 mn as opposed to only £14·5 mn. It is against this larger amount that surplus value must be set in calculating the rate of profit: £9 mn : £27 mn, which gives a rate of profit over six years of only 33 per cent (as opposed to 62·4 per cent in the car industry) and an annual rate of profit of 5·5 per cent (compared with 10·4 per cent).[15] These differences in the rate of profit can be understood in another way. To double production the car producer and the shipbuilder need different amounts of capital: £14·5 mn and £27 mn respectively. Yet at the end of six years' production both have exactly the same amount of surplus value at their disposal to finance new investment. The differences in the rate of expansion they can achieve is entirely due to differences in turnover.

We know:

$$p' = \frac{s}{K + c' + v} \tag{1}$$

where, p' represents the rate of profit gained during one turnover of circulating capital.

Assuming that all circulating capital turns over at the same rate:

$$t^v = t^{c'}$$

$$c' = C\frac{t^{c'}}{t^c} = C\frac{t^v}{t^c}$$

$$v = V\frac{t^v}{t^c}$$

and

$$s = S\frac{t^v}{t^c}$$

∴

$$p' = \frac{S\dfrac{t^v}{t^o}}{K + C'\dfrac{t^v}{t^c} + V\dfrac{t^v}{t^c}} \tag{2}$$

and

$$P' = \frac{S\dfrac{t^v}{t^c}}{K + C'\dfrac{t^v}{t^c} + V\dfrac{t^v}{t^c}}\frac{t^c}{t^v}$$

---

[15] This example must not be taken literally, for, in so far as the difference in the rate of profit is due to differences in the organic composition of production it will be evened out by the transformation of values into prices of production in the formation of an average rate of profit. Within branches, however, profits are not evened out in this way so a lower organic

$$= \frac{S}{K + C' \dfrac{t^v}{t^c} + V \dfrac{t^v}{t^c}} \tag{3}$$

where P' represents the total rate of profit gained during the lifetime of fixed capital.

From equation (3) in particular, it is clear that the higher the ratio $t^c : t^v$, or conversely, the lower the ratio $t^v : t^c$, the lower are C' and V and therefore the higher is the rate of profit. In general the rate of profit on any capital will rise with an increase in relative turnover given the organic composition of the commodity even where the rate of surplus value remains constant.

For this reason it is always to the interest of capital to increase relative turnover by as much as it can on every possible occasion. But, since, as we have seen any increase in this ratio causes the organic composition of production to rise relatively to the organic composition of the commodity, there must always be present in the process of accumulation an inherent tendency for this one aspect of the organic accumulation of capital to rise relatively to the other. In other words, as the process of accumulation goes on, the capital composition of production tends to rise relatively to the capital composition of the commodity. We shall call this *the relative rise* in the organic composition of production, to distinguish it from an *absolute rise* in the organic composition of production which affects the rate of profit in exactly the opposite way.

The force that brings about the absolute rise in the organic composition of production originates from the very heart of the process of accumulation itself. In the last analysis accumulation is determined by the rate of surplus value, the ratio of paid to unpaid labour. And, as we have seen, this, in turn, is determined by the productivity of labour, which, other things being equal, is greater when workers are well equipped with instruments of labour. Thus to the extent that an absolute rise in the

---

composition of production brought about through an increase in relative turnover will lead to higher rates of profit. Furthermore, any increase in relative turnover will benefit all capital by increasing the average rate of profit.

organic composition of production brings this about, it leads directly to a rise in the rate of surplus value and also to an increase in the rate of profit. But, at the same time, it has indirect effects that tend to depress profitability.

In order to simplify the analysis without changing its essential features we can leave the materials of labour C' out of account. If we start by assuming the ratio $t^v : t^c = 1$, so that the two aspects of the organic composition of capital discussed so far equal each other, we can define the rate of profit in conventional terms as:

$$p' = \frac{s}{c + v}$$

From this it is possible to derive an alternative formula:

$$p' = \frac{s}{v} \div \left(1 + \frac{c}{v}\right)$$

where the rate of profit shows itself clearly as a ratio with the rate of surplus value in the numerator and the organic composition of capital in the denominator. A rise in the rate of surplus value thus causes the rate of profit to go up; a rise in the organic composition of capital causes it to come down; and any rise in the rate of profit brought about by an increase in the rate of surplus value achieved through an increase in the mechanisation of production must be offset by the depressing effects this has through increasing the organic composition of capital. In practice, the rate of profit can move in either direction. If the rate of surplus value rises sufficiently it cannot only offset the depressing effects of a rising organic composition of capital, but can bring about an actual rise in the rate of profit. But even where this happens, *the law of the falling rate of profit* due to a rising organic composition of capital is not invalidated, for it is a tendential law of capitalist development not an empirical forecast. It operates independently of what happens to the rate of surplus value, since in all circumstances it tends to bring the rate of profit down below what would otherwise be the case. Its depressing effects upon profitability are always present as a constraint upon accumulation which capital can never eliminate but which it can hold at bay.

To take account of relative turnover we need to modify this formula so that:

$$P' = \frac{S}{V\dfrac{t^c}{t^v}} \div \left(1 + \frac{K}{V\dfrac{t^c}{t^v}} \right)$$

Again both numerator and denominator are affected by the change in opposite directions. An increase in relative turnover shown here by a fall in the ratio $t^v : t^c$ tends to increase the rate of profit in so far as it increases $S/(Vt^v/t^c)$ and reduces it in so far as it brings about a rise in the organic composition of production. But the net effect is *always* positive for the rate of profit.

We can now distinguish between an absolute rise in the organic composition of production and a relative rise, and the corresponding effect of each upon the rate of profit more precisely. An absolute rise takes place when K/V rises due to an increase in K or a fall in V, or both simultaneously. A relative rise takes place when v falls due to an increase in the rate of turnover of circulating capital in relation to that of fixed capital. Or to put it another way: the organic composition of production increases in absolute terms when the amount of constant capital employed rises in relation to the amount of variable capital employed. When the organic composition of capital rises only relatively, the amounts of constant and variable capital employed remain the same, but the amount of variable capital advanced falls.

The distinction between absolute and relative increases in the organic composition production can also be seen through the effects they have upon the rate of surplus value. In the first case, the rate of surplus value rises to the extent that exploitation increases due to a rise in productivity; but, as we have noted, this increase may or may not be sufficient to offset the depressing effects of the absolute rise in the organic composition of production that brought it about. In the second case, the real rate of exploitation remains the same – i.e. the same proportion of the new value produced by labour is appropriated by capital – but the rate of surplus per unit of time increases. Or to put it another way: the rate of surplus value on variable capital employed, the *real* rate of surplus value, remains constant; but the rate of surplus value on variable capital advanced goes up.[16] And because of the nature of the rate of profit it always goes up sufficiently to more than offset the depressing effects of the relative rise in the organic composition of production associated with it.

At first sight the increase in the rate of profit that comes through an increase in relative turnover seems to invalidate the law of value, for given the fact the rate of surplus value has been assumed constant throughout, the additional profitability seems to have been conjured from the sphere of circulation. But on close inspection all the mystery that surrounds this increased profitability disappears. Firstly, changes in the relative turnover do not affect the actual amounts of capital employed in the process of production, nor the ratios in which they are employed. Secondly, the absolute amount of surplus value and profit remains unchanged and equal to the unrewarded product of labour. All that happens as relative turnover increases is that the amount of capital *advanced* falls and it is this fall alone that is responsible for the increase in the rate of profit.

3. *Turnover and employment*

In section 2 of this chapter, it was claimed that the organic composition of production was a better indicator of the effects of accumulation on employment than the organic composition of the commodity, because it made the distinction between fixed and circulating capital explicit. It shows, to take car production as an example, that while all fixed capital is fully active in a material form for the whole of its lifetime, only a proportion of the total variable capital employed functions each year. Over six years the firm employs £9 mn variable capital which, on the basis of the assumptions made in Chapter 2, offers employment to 9000 workers. But each year it employs only £1·5 mn, of variable capital and consequently offers jobs to only 1500 workers. From the point of view of the level of employment this lower figure is the more significant, and therefore, the organic composition of production is a more accurate guide to the effects of accumulation on employment than the organic

---

[16] See Marx, *Capital*, vol. 2, chapter XV.

composition of the commodity. Yet it is not perfectly reliable.

Its shortcomings in this context arise from the fact that when it increases relatively due to a rise in the rate of relative turnover the level of employment does not necessarily fall as one might expect. The comparison of car manufacturing and shipbuilding used in the last section makes this abundantly clear. It will be recalled that in constructing this example we assumed production in the two branches identical in every respect except the nature of the product and the rate at which it could be sold. The consequence of this was to make the organic composition of production in the car industry equal to 8·6 as opposed to 2 in shipbuilding: the difference being directly attributable to the difference in relative turnover. But while this has definite effects on the rate of profit by changing the amount of capital advanced in the two industries, it has no impact whatsoever on the number of jobs offered. This is determined by the amount of variable capital employed which is the same in both industries, despite the fact that one advances a much greater amount than the other. In concrete terms, given the wage rate, it is the value of variable capital employed that determines employment and it makes no difference to the workers whether they are paid out of new advances or capital recycled from a previous turnover period. In fact, an increase in the organic composition of production brought about by a rise in relative turnover, will, if anything, lead to an increase in employment in so far as it brings about an increase in the rate of profit and the greater accumulation resulting from this creates new jobs.

In one sense these difficulties are of a minor technical nature which can be dealt with quite easily. At the same time they raise a fundamental question about the relationship between accumulation and employment. This cannot be seen, however, until the technical details are cleared up.

Consider the definition of the organic composition of production as
$$\frac{c\dfrac{t^c}{t^v}+c'}{v} \quad \text{or more simply} \quad \frac{K+C'}{V\dfrac{t^v}{t^c}}$$

It is the organic composition of the commodity modified to take account of relative turnover. But, although relative turnover

tells us how much capital is advanced and is therefore appropriate for calculating the rate of profit, it does not tell us how
much capital actually functions in the sphere of production at
any one time and therefore cannot give a direct indication of
employment. A turnover of capital, it will be recalled, consists
of the series of changes in form that capital undergoes as it
moves from one phase in its circuit back to that *same* phase.
Thus the turnover of circulating capital, of which variable
capital is a key component can be described as:

$$P' \dots C' - M' - C_{MP}^{L} \dots P'$$

where P' represents circulating capital. The time this takes
is called the period of turnover, which we assumed was equal
to one year in the car industry and six years in shipbuilding.
But circulating capital and therefore variable capital are forms
of productive capital and can only function as such when they
are actually engaged in the sphere of production. Once variable
capital has left this sphere, even as soon as gets as far as C', it
ceases to be capital in production and becomes capital in
circulation: in other words it no longer functions as variable
capital. Thus when we wish to consider the amount of variable
capital actually employed in production it is not the time it
takes this capital actually to complete its circuit that counts,
but the time it takes it to quit the sphere of production. In
other words it is the time it takes to pass from $P \dots C'$ that
matters, not the period of turnover which is the time it takes to
pass from $P \dots P$. In this respect, conditions in car production and
shipbuilding are identical. It is true that in the car industry
variable capital is able to complete its whole circuit within a
year, while in shipbuilding it cannot move so fast. But nevertheless in the shipbuilding industry it does leave the sphere of
production and gets as far as C' in the same time, and therefore
no longer functions as variable capital. For this reason both
industries actually employ the same amount of variable capital
at the same time, despite the fact that in one industry it turns
over six times rapidly as in the other.

To clarify the matter in formal terms we need to define a
third aspect of the organic composition of capital, namely the

organic composition of productive capital which equals

$$\frac{K+C\dfrac{f^v}{f^c}}{V\dfrac{f^v}{f^c}}$$

where f^c is the time it takes fixed constant capital to quit the sphere of production, and f^v the time it takes circulating capital to do the same. In both the car and the shipbuilding industries $f^c = 6$ years and $f^v = 1$, so that given the common values of 12 mn K, 6 mn C' and 9 mn V, the organic composition of productive capital is equal to 8·6 in both branches, (i.e. 13 : 1·5). In other words, for every £14·5 mn of capital actually employed in the process of production during one year only £1·5 mn is variable capital used to employ labour.

4. *Accumulation and employment*

Assuming the value of the wage constant, the organic composition of productive capital is the best indicator we have for effects of accumulation on employment defined in a conventional sense, for it gives an exact measure of the proportion of capital that actually functions as variable capital in the sphere of production. As it rises, other things being equal, employment falls. In a situation where it is equal to 1, £50 of each £100 of productive capital functions as variable capital and is used to employ workers. If it rises to 4 only £20 will function in this way and employment drops correspondingly. Of course, if productive capital accumulates two and a half times while the organic composition of production rises at this rate, the absolute amount of functioning variable capital remains constant and employment will not fall. If accumulation is faster employment will actually rise.[17]

But employment, as we talk of it here, refers only to employment at a moment in time; that is, to the number of jobs in

---

[17] If the value of the wage falls due to a cheapening of commodities in general and labour-power in particular, then any reduction in the absolute amount of variable capital employed will have a less depressing effect on employment. Thus if the value of labour-power and the wage halves while variable capital halves employment will remain constant: if the value of labour-power falls faster, employment will rise.

current existence. And although this is the sense in which the term is commonly understood, and the one that has most meaning for the working class, it is not the only sense that can be given to it. Nor is it the aspect of employment which primarily concerns capital.

Consider the conventional definition of the organic composition of capital, the organic composition of the commodity, K/V. This also gives a measure of variable capital as the proportion of total capital, and given the sum of capital employed we can derive with its use the amount of variable capital employed. If it has a value of 1 and capital employed is equal to £100, then variable capital will equal £50. And just as the absolute amount of variable capital and employment varies with the rate of accumulation and the organic composition of productive capital, so it also varies with the rate of accumulation and the organic composition of the commodity. Thus both these aspects of the organic composition of capital give an indication of the effects of accumulation on employment, but with one important difference: the aspect of employment they refer to is different. Whereas the organic composition of productive capital relates to the number of workers actually in jobs at a moment in time; the organic composition of the commodity relates to the number of workers employed during the total lifetime of the plant. In formal terms the difference between these two aspects of employment, one of which can be called *current employment, e,* and the other, *long-term employment, E,* can be defined as:

$$\frac{e}{E} = \frac{c}{v\dfrac{f^c}{f^v}} : \frac{v}{c}$$

$$= \frac{f^v}{f^c}$$

In words, the difference between them is equal to the ratio of the working periods of constant and variable capital: the higher this ratio, the lower is current employment relative to long-term employment.

There are two reasons to expect f^v/f^c to rise with accumulation and so depress current employment in relative terms. First, although a rise in relative turnover does not lead automatically to a rise in f^v/f^c since the shortening of the turnover period of variable capital can be achieved by speeding up circulation rather than production – relative turnover is higher in car manufacturing than shipbuilding for this reason: an increase in f^v/f^c will almost inevitably increase relative turnover. And to the extent that it does this tends to increase the rate of profit. The second reason is more complex and is directly relevant to the question of industrial employment in the underdeveloped world.

In order to increase the rate of surplus value capital works continuously to increase the productivity of labour by improving and increasing the means of production at the disposal of the workforce. In concrete terms this means increasing the amount of fixed capital in relation to the number of workers in current employment – i.e. increasing the organic composition of productive capital. At the same time capital is concerned to keep the ratio of fixed capital to long-term employment as low as possible for, given any rate of relative turnover, a rise here tends to lower the rate of profit. In formal terms, it does this by increasing the organic composition of the commodity and production. But we can understand this in less formal terms that are more evidently relevant to the question of employment. As the organic composition of capital rises in all its aspects, variable capital falls relatively to total capital, which means that mass of labour employed relative to constant capital falls. In other words, the personal agent of production which alone is capable of creating new value and surplus value plays, quantitatively speaking, a smaller part in the process of production. The basis on which profit is produced is narrowed. But if f^v/f^c rises capital cannot only check this movement but it can simultaneously achieve a higher degree of mechanisation and exploitation. On the one hand it can increase the mass of the means of production at the disposal of its labour force, both by increasing this mass absolutely and by reducing the number of workers in current employment. On the other it can keep the fall in long-term unemployment under control.

To illustrate how this affects employment assume a situation in which $K = 60$, $V = 40$, $f^c/f^v = 2$, and each unit of variable capital offers employment to 1 worker. Then:

the organic composition of the commodity $=\dfrac{K}{V}=1\cdot 5$

the organic composition of productive capital $=\dfrac{K}{V\dfrac{f_v}{f_c}}=3$

long-term employment, $E=40$

current employment, $e=20$

Now suppose the organic composition of the commodity changes so that $K=80$ and $V=20$ and at the same time f^v/f^c rises to 4. Now:

the organic composition of the commodity $=\dfrac{K}{V}=4$

the organic composition of productive capital $=\dfrac{K}{V\dfrac{f_c}{f_v}}=16$

long-term employment, $E=20$

current employment, $e=5$

Contrasting the two situations we can see that the effect of doubling the organic composition of capital and the ratio f^v/f^c leads to a fourfold drop in current employment but to only a halving of long-term employment.

Thus the logic of accumulation, in so far as it increases the ratio f^v/f^c is to reduce current employment relative to long-term employment. The strategy of capital is to intensify the exploitation of relatively fewer workers at any moment in time, while attempting to keep as many workers as possible in employment over the long period. Moreover, it pays capital to adopt this strategy irrespective of relative supplies of factors of production: in other words it pays to adopt it as much in the underdeveloped countries where the pool of unemployed workers is much greater than in the developed countries.

It is true that a rise in the ratio f^c/f^v leads to a variation of short- and long-term employment only relatively to each other, and does not determine the axis about which this variation takes place, namely the organic composition of the commodity. For example, if f^c/f^v is equal to 4, long-term employment will be four times greater than current employment whatever the value of the organic composition of capital, although both will be absolutely greater the lower this value. Assuming this value of $f^c/f^v = 4$, and that one unit of variable capital offers employment for 1 man, consider two situations; one where $K/V = 20/80$ and another where it equals $80/20$. In the first case current employment is 20 and long-term employment 80; in the latter the values are 5 and 20 respectively. In other words, the ratio between the two aspects of employment is the same in both cases, but the absolute levels of employment differ, according to the ratios of the organic composition of the commodity. In this light, it could be claimed, the ratio f^c/f^c is of only secondary importance compared with the size of the organic composition of the commodity, and that it is perfectly consistent for capital in the underdeveloped world to do everything it can to increase this ratio while keeping the organic composition of the commodity down to take advantage of the plentiful supplies of labour.

On the other hand, however, there are powerful theoretical reasons for believing that capital will not choose techniques with an organic composition of the commodity low enough to offer current employment to all workers in the underdeveloped world in the way the neo-classical economists believe it should. First, f^c/f^v tends to rise with the organic composition of the commodity so that more mechanised techniques can actually generate more long-term employment than less mechanised alternatives. Taking two situations where $C/(Vf^v/f^c) = 20/80$, and $80/20$, and each unit of variable capital offers employment to 1 man, assume that f^c/f^v equals only 1 in the first case but $0 \cdot 1$ in the second. In the first case long-term employment equals 80, while in the second case it equals 100. In other words, the more mechanised technique of production which only offers one-quarter of the current employment of the less mechanised one, makes a more plentiful use of labour in the long period, and is therefore the more rational one for capital to adopt in the underdeveloped countries even by neo-classical criteria. Second, to the extent that mechanisation increases productivity and therefore the rate of exploitation it is always potentially a profitable course of action. Of course the rise in the organic composition of capital associated with it tends to depress the rate of profit, but this factor is not peculiar to the underdeveloped countries. Third, an increase in f^c/f^v increases the rate of profit in so far as it increases relative turnover and this will tend to bias capital towards greater mechanisation.

It is no part of this argument that the reserve army of labour in the underdeveloped world pays no role in determining the pattern of technical development and that it always pays capital to use the most mechanised techniques at its command. It is a more modest point that needs to be established: even in conditions of large-scale unemployment the very logic of accumulation makes the choice of techniques of production which offer jobs to only a limited section of the available proletariat a rational course of action. Capital has no economic imperative, let alone a moral one, to create full employment. The actual degree of mechanisation it chooses and the number of people it leaves jobless will depend upon the interplay of all the factors mentioned above. All that can be said theoretically is that the rationality of accumulation does not preclude sufficient mechanisation and the build-up of large-scale unemployment – a conclusion which is perfectly consistent with the trend of actual events.

Thus mechanisation and unemployment in the underdeveloped world cannot be ascribed to imperfections of the capitalist process in the way that neo-classical economists suggest; nor can they be put down simply to the dependence of the underdeveloped countries on the developed ones for their machine tools. It is a *normal* feature of capitalist development, and as such, is independent of any particular form of ownership or dependence. It is just as profitable for local capitalists to adopt techniques of production that fail to absorb all the available labour as it is for international firms: even if the underdeveloped countries produced their own machine tools instead of importing them from the developed world, it would still pay them to aim for relatively mechanised technology. For all these reasons unemployment in the underdeveloped world is not a problem amenable to solution by reforms such as perfecting factor markets – i.e. reducing wages; localising key sectors of production; expelling foreign firms or developing some form of intermediate technology.

5. *The formation of the proletariat*

The level of unemployment depends as much upon the numbers seeking jobs as upon the number of jobs that capital makes available, though this aspect of the question receives relatively less attention in the literature on unemployment in the underdeveloped world. One reason is that it is not easily amenable to change by policy. In so far as it is due to the size and growth of population in general, measures to control population can achieve nothing in the short period – the workers who will be unemployed in twenty years' time are already born. On the other hand to leave this aspect of the matter out of consideration is to come close to a tacit acceptance that it is a natural problem; whereas, in fact, the forces that determine the size of the proletariat are as integral to capitalist development as those that determine the degree of mechanisation and the scale of employment. In so far as the growth of population is responsible for the problem, capital itself has already claimed the credit. Apologists for colonialism have not been backward in insisting that the changes colonial governments brought about – such as the establishment of law and order and the ending of local warfare; the construction of transport systems that allowed food to be imported into areas of dearth; the establishment of modern health and education facilities – played a key role in reducing the death rate. The fall in *per capita* food production in India in the first half of this century shows that many of these claims are hypocritical, to say the least. Yet it is a generally observable fact that population does grow with capitalist penetration and it would be difficult to deny some relationship between them.

The point is not worth pursuing in detail, for it is the social composition of a population rather than its size which is important in this context.[18] Thus China with the largest population in the world and with a density of population comparable with that of India is not afflicted with the problem. Even in those parts of the underdeveloped world where the pressure of population on the land is not that great, heavy urban unemployment already exists and is growing rapidly. The growth of population obviously plays a part in the formation of a prole-

---

[18] In starting an analysis 'it seems correct to begin with the real and concrete, with the real precondition, thus to begin, in economics, with e.g. the population, which is the foundation and the subject of the entire social act of production. However, on closer examination, this proves false. The population is an abstraction if I leave out, for example, the classes of which it is composed' (Marx, *Grundrisse*, p. 100).

tariat but it is the social processes whereby large sections of the community are separated from their means of production that is the decisive factor.

The means whereby this separation has been effected, and is still continuing, vary from one part of the underdeveloped world to the next. In some areas it was achieved by direct means such as depriving peasants the use of land and driving people from the countryside by the establishment of a capitalist mode of production in agriculture. In other areas, colonial governments did everything they could to protect local land rights and prevent the formation of a proletariat. For this reason generalisations must be hazardous. But there is one feature common to all parts of the underdeveloped world – the encouragement of commodity production.

We have seen that merchant capital can function in any mode of production so long as a significant part of the social product takes the form of commodities. To this extent its existence does not require a proletariat. On the contrary, in so far as the very existence of a proletariat is associated with industrial capital, it is inconsistent with merchant capital in its independent form, which, together with its political representatives, will go to considerable lengths to retard its formation. Nevertheless the development of commodity production which merchant capital must necessarily foster inevitably corrodes the pre-capitalist social formations in which it operates. The monetisation of the economy that necessarily follows in its wake undermines existing systems of property relations and introduces new criteria into the process of production itself. Its arrival in a society where production is solely for use must bring about a change in practice. The introduction of production for exchange opens new possibilities and establishes new criteria of efficiency. Patterns of production that previously passed unquestioned dissolve in the market place. Property relations that have been accepted for centuries become an obstacle to the new rationality of the law of value that merchant capital seeks to impose, and relations of private property spring up in their place. These changes do not lead directly and inevitably to the formation of a proletariat. In Britain, for example, they were taking place on a substantial scale as early as the sixteenth century but the modern working class did not emerge until late in the eighteenth century. But they do establish the pre-conditions for this development by shaking the ties that link producers directly to their means of production.

But merchant capital did more in the underdeveloped world than undermining traditional relations of production in the countryside. It established commercial centres in the major cities which acted like magnetic poles drawing labour out of the rural areas even when few jobs were available. The educational system it set up to provide literacy for its clerical workers offered the possibility of social advancement to sections of the community who found their way blocked at home. The local response to its initiatives was often much greater than merchant capital might have wished, but once it had set a process of social decomposition in motion it was in no position to check its progress.

The collapse of the system of colonial trade in the thirties ruined many producers who had become dependent upon it driving them, or their children, to search for new jobs in the towns. At the same time it created the possibility for a reorganisation of agricultural production. The result was that by the end of the Second World War the formation of a considerable proletariat was well under way in most parts of the underdeveloped world. It is true that this development did not compare in size or intensity with what happened in Britain at the end of the eighteenth century, but it happened one hundred and fifty years later in a totally different economic context, where the forces of production were far more advanced. If, as is sometimes suggested, nineteenth-century techniques were widely adopted in the underdeveloped world it is possible that industrial capital would be able to absorb much of its labour at its disposal. But as these techniques are not the most profitable, this is really beside the point. The harsh fact is that the techniques which are profitable do not require the labour that presents itself at the factory doors; and given the real possibility of even greater mechanisation in the future, coupled with an even larger rural exodus, the prospects of any reduction in unemployment seem bleak. It is likely that in ten years time the present rate of unemployment will be viewed with a certain nostalgia as a sign of good times unlikely to return.

7. The Acceleration of Capital

As capital accumulates it increases not only the rate of exploitation but also its rate of turnover. While the former is obscured by rising real wages the effects of the latter are plainly visible and directly experienced by all sections of the society. Their impact on the sphere of consumption has always evoked traditional conservative complaints about a 'decline in the quality of life' which in recent years have swollen into a fashionable torrent of radical criticism. Capital is intoxicated with speed just as much as with quantity: the question how much? always implies another, how quickly? The 'increase in the pace of life' which so many commentators bemoan and explain in terms of the means by which it is achieved – i.e. in terms of modern technology or some other facile euphemism – is the visible result of increases in the rate of turnover of capital for the sole purpose of increasing surplus value and accumulation.

1. *The intensification of labour*

In the last chapter we saw that the rate of profit rose with an increase in relative turnover – i.e. the turnover of circulating capital in relation to that of fixed capital. Now we must consider *absolute turnover* – the turnover of capital as a whole – for this affects the rate of profit in much the same way. Consider:

$$p' = \frac{P'}{y}$$

where p' represents the annual rate of profit; P', the rate of profit over the life of fixed capital: and y, this period measured in years. As a reduction in y must increase the annual rate of profit, it is clear the rate of accumulation depends not only upon how much surplus value capital can extract from labour but how quickly it can extract it. Suppose a capital of £1000 is able to gather £200 surplus value during its lifetime which gives it an overall rate of profit, P', of 20 per cent. If this lifetime is five years the annual rate of profit and therefore the maximum annual rate of accumulation is 4 per cent; reducing it to one year increases the possible rate of accumulation to 20 per cent. Thus there is a most powerful inducement for capital not only to speed up the turnover of circulation capital relative to that of fixed capital, but to speed up the turnover of fixed capital itself. For capital time is indeed money.

Historically the first decisive efforts to capitalise time came in the field of transport, for improvements here increase the rate of turnover as well as reducing the cost-price of production. Capital is value in perpetual motion, and the speed with which it can convert itself from one form to the next is the essence of the matter. But paradoxically the time when the commodities it produces are in physical motion from factories to consumers, is one of immobility from the point of view of value. For during this period capital is stuck in its commodity form and unable to convert itself into money. Furthermore, the longer this period lasts, the greater is the amount of capital any given level of value production requires. Leaving aside the question of relative turnover, assume a situation where a capital of £1000, which gathers surplus value of £500, can pass through the first three stages of its circuit in one week, but takes three weeks to complete the final lap because of poor transport:
i.e.

$$M - C_{MP}{}^{L}... P - C' \text{ takes one week}$$
but $\quad C' - M' \text{ takes three weeks}$
where $M = £1000$ and $C' = M' = £1500$.

To keep the process of production moving continuously in these conditions a firm requires capital of £4000. During the first month of its operations it must advance £1000 afresh each week since it is unable to realise anything from the sale of its products. Thereafter it is better off to the extent that it has a steady return and does not need to pump in new capital; on the other hand, it always has three weeks' output with a value of £4500 in transit. Of this two-thirds, £3000, represents advanced capital and together with the £1000 currently operating in the sphere of production, this makes up the same sum of £4000 of necessary advances. To calculate the rate of profit this sum must be set against the amount of surplus value it realises as money each month. After the first month, it realises surplus value at the rate of £500 a week, so that its rate of profit per month is 50 per cent.

Now assume an improvement in transport cuts transit time to a week so that:

$$M - C_{MP}^L \dots P \dots C' \text{ takes one week}$$
and $\quad C' - M'$ also takes one week

with M and C' remaining the same at £1000 and £1500 respectively. Capital requirements are now sharply reduced as there is never more than one week's production worth £1500 in transit, of which £1000 together with the other £1000 operating in the process of production, makes a total advance of £2000, a reduction of 50 per cent. As absolute surplus value remains the same, the rate of profit is 100 per cent. As a general rule the rate of profit rises, other things being equal, in strict proportion to a fall in the period of turnover: here this period has halved from four to two weeks and the rate of profit doubled.

Except for those heavy goods such as coal and steel where transport costs make up a high percentage of total costs, improved transport has done more to increase profitability by reducing the period of turnover than by actually reducing costs per ton mile. Speed, that was the great contribution of the railway and steamship in the nineteenth century. As late as 1850 in Britain it is possible that a relatively inexpensive reorganisation of the canal system could have made it competitive with railways in costs per ton mile, but it could never possibly have competed for speed. Now that the railway itself is being surpassed it is difficult to appreciate the major breakthrough it was; in the field of commercial transport nothing of comparable significance had been achieved this century. Efforts to speed the turnover of capital have been mainly directed to the sphere of production itself.

Consider a situation where production takes three weeks and a further week is then needed to get the goods to consumers. For simplicity, assume that all capital has to be advanced on the first day of production and that M and C' are again equal to £1000 and £1500 respectively. The situation is thus the reverse of the one first considered above in that:

$$M - C_{MP}^L \dots P \dots C' \text{ takes three weeks}$$
and $\quad C' - M'$ takes one week.

But as it still takes four weeks for capital as a whole to complete its circuit, the rate of profit equals 50 per cent per month. If the period of production is reduced to one week the turnover period of capital is halved, and other things being equal, the rate of profit rises to 100 per cent per month in exactly the same way as when time was saved by shortening the period of transit. From the point of view of the rate of profit the manner in which time is saved is immaterial and speed-ups in the sphere of circulation have exactly the same effects on speed-ups in the sphere of production. On the other hand a speed-up in the sphere of production does have special implications that are hidden by the direct effects it has on profitability. Here, in particular, we have an instance of an example whose very arithmetic simplicity obscures as much as it reveals. We must therefore examine it in close detail.

It is clear that the rate of profit can only rise in strict proportion to the shortening of the turnover period of capital if all the values of the various elements in the circuit of capital remain unchanged during the speed-up. A single change in any one of them will break this strict proportionality unless it is compensated for in an arbitrary way by a whole series of other changes. For instance, assume that when production takes three weeks the organic composition of capital equals 1; so that:

$$500c + 500v + 500s = 1500C'$$

As it takes one month for capital to turnover, the monthly rate of profit is 50 per cent. Now assume production is speeded up by reducing the number of workers and providing more equipment – a strategy we can depict by assuming a rise in the organic composition of capital, from 1 to, say, 1·6. If production under these new conditions still employs the same amount of capital, we now have:

$$600c + 400v + 400s = 1400C'$$

The rate of surplus value is the same at 100 per cent, but the rate of profit per turnover falls to 40 per cent. On the other hand the period of turnover is now only two weeks so that the £1000 advanced is recovered in a fortnight and can be employed twice in a month. This takes the monthly rate of profit up to 80 per cent which although higher than the original 50 per cent is nevertheless lower than the 100 per cent previously achieved by a similar speed-up. In other words, we no longer have a strictly proportionality between the increase in the rate of profit and the shortening of the period of turnover that has brought it about. The reason for this is clearly the depressing effect that the rise in the organic composition of capital has upon the rate of profit. At the same time, another change has taken place: the value of production has fallen from £1500 to £1400. This is a vital clue since it shows that what we are dealing with here is a case of increased productivity. And it follows that where a speed-up of production is achieved through an increase in the productivity of labour, which, in turn, is brought about by a rise in the organic composition of capital, the rate of profit can only go up by an equal proportion to a shortening of the period of turnover of capital, arbitrary compensatory changes occur in the value of capital advanced and the rate of surplus value.

In one sense, it can be argued, this strict proportionality does not matter, for capital increases its rate of profit and this is all that counts. On the other hand, the question of strict proportionality still remains. Nor can it be dismissed as simply formalistic since it has important real implications which might escape the observer but cannot fail to strike the worker.

We know that if the rate of profit rises at exactly the same rate as the turnover period of capital shortens, and we do not permit a number of arbitrary changes to take place in the value of capital advanced and the rate of surplus value, the size and composition of capital must remain unchanged throughout the speed-up. Here this means that the process of production that previously took three weeks must be compressed into a single week without any other changes at all taking place. That is to say, one week's production must be:

$$500c + 500v + 500s = 1500C'$$

But at first sight this seems impossible. If we deliberately leave aside the possibility of extra work time through night shifts, we appear to have an irreconcilable contradiction on our hands. For whichever way one looks at it, compressing three weeks' production into one must mean a reduction in the number of hours of labour expended in production. Suppose that 8 men are employed for a 40-hour week; then three weeks' production consumes 960 hours of living labour. If we now exclude the possibility on technical grounds of employing more workers, compressing production into one week must reduce this figure to 320. And this in turn must surely reduce the value produced; for while labour might be capable of trebling its material output per hour – i.e. increasing its productivity – it cannot increase the value of what it produces in an hour. For an hour of labour is the measure of value: or so it appears!

The solution to this problem is deceptively simple: an hour's labour where production lasts one week is not the same as an hour's labour where production takes three weeks. It is labour *intensified* to the power three. By analogy: just as a ton of steel is denser than a ton of feathers, so one hour's labour can be denser than another, and the value produced during this denser hour is correspondingly greater!

> This condensation of a greater mass of labour into a given period... counts for what really is a greater quantity of labour. In addition to its measure of extension, i.e. duration, labour now acquires a measure of its intensity or of the degree of its condensation or density. The denser hour ... [when production is compressed into a single week] ... contains more labour, i.e. expended labour-power, than the more porous hour ... [of three weeks' production]. The product therefore of one of the former hours has as much value as the product of [three] of the latter hours.[1]

The process whereby the value produced in a single hour is increased in this way is called the *intensification of labour* and it plays a vital part not only in speed-up but in capitalist development as a whole.

In practice it is extremely difficult to distinguish an intensification of labour from an increase in productivity, at least, through the medium of an 'objective' indicator. Firstly the two go together; in most cases labour is intensified through an increase in mechanisation which simultaneously increases its productivity. And it is always difficult to distinguish, in practice, between two processes that advance together with apparently identical results. Secondly, an intensification of labour

[1] Marx, *Capital*, vol. 1, pp. 408–9.

will show up as increase in productivity in so far as one of its results in an increase in the rate of material production per unit of time. Suppose in our example C' whose value was £1500 consisted of 1920 yards of cloth. When production takes three weeks and consumes 960 hours of labour, output per man hour is 2 yards. When the period of production is reduced and contains only 320 man hours, output per hour rises to 6 yards. Here apparently is a clear unambiguous indicator of increased productivity and the academic economist who believes in such objectivity will feel that nothing further needs to be said. For him, the idea of intensified labour and a constant level of value production behind the increase in material production appears 'metaphysical'. It has no objective indicator like productivity that can be measured in terms of material otuput per man hour. The worker, however, knows better: he experiences intensification directly as more effort, more concentration, more exhaustion. In a word he experiences if for what it really is – more work! The economist who rejects this as subjectivism and believes that truth is to be found in government statistics on productivity is encouraged to spend eight hours on a modern conveyor-belt and then argue the toss on whether he really is tired or only feels that way.

In theory the distinction between increased productivity and intensification is clear-cut. Both resound to the advantage of capital, but they do so in different ways. A general increase in productivity increases the rate of surplus value by reducing the value of labour-power along with that of all other commodities. The effect of an intensification of labour on the rate of surplus value is more complex. In the first instance the value of commodities is not affected and this can leave the value of labour-power and the rate of surplus value unchanged. The value of the hourly wage goes up, but on the other hand the amount of labour-power the worker sells per hour also increases. More work means more wear and tear on the worker who needs to consume more to keep fit and active. An obvious example is the heavy manual worker who requires more food than someone performing much lighter labour. However, there is no reason for the increase in the value of labour-power, and hence the wage, to be as great as the increase in intensity; certainly it is to the interests of capital for it to increase more slowly, for this will cause a rise in the rate of surplus value. In our example, when production takes three weeks, capital purchases 960 hours of labour-power for £500 giving an hourly wage rate of a shade over 52p per hour. If the intensification of labour as much as doubles the value of labour-power capital still benefits, for its total wage-bill is only £312·80 – i.e. 320 hours at £1·04 per hour. Surplus value rises absolutely from £500 to £687·20, so the rate of surplus value goes up from 100 to 219 per cent per month and the rate of profit rises from 50 to just over 152 per cent per month. It is true that if this happens strict proportionality between the fall in the rate of turnover of capital and the rise in the rate of profit does not hold, but the reason for this is apparent and there is no hidden condition that needs seeking out. The intensification of labour increases the rate of profit in two ways, by increasing the absolute amount of surplus value and reducing the period of its production and realisation.

Leaving aside for the moment the effects of increasing productivity which can reduce the value of labour-power directly, the intensification of labour makes possible what is apparently paradoxical: namely an increase in the value of the wage alongside a rising rate of surplus value and profit. It is undoubtedly one of the main factors that have allowed a rise in real wages and working class living standards in this century. On the one hand this increased rate of consumption is a gain for labour; on the other, capital also benefits by increasing the rate of exploitation and shortening the time it takes to extract its surplus value. In our example, allowing for the fact that the value of labour-power rises less quickly than intensification, the value of the monthly wage rises from £666.60 to £1251.20, as the period of production falls from three weeks to one week. At the same time two other developments occur. Firstly, the share of labour, $v/(c+s)$, falls from 50 per cent to just over 26 per cent; but, secondly, the level of material output rises threefold. Thus if we set the level of original production at 100, the intensification of labour causes material production to rise to 400. The result is a rise in the level of working class consumption per month from 50 to 104, i.e. it increases by 108 per cent. But even this gain of the working class can be illusory.

Consider the two ways in which consumption can rise. First, there can be an increase in the actual amount of commodities purchased so that at any one point in time there are indeed more goods in current use. In this case the level of consumption clearly does rise. But secondly it is possible for the number of goods in current use to remain constant, if the useful life of each falls and a correspondingly greater amount have to be purchased. Take a concrete example: a doubling in the consumption of ladies tights can be brought about either by customers buying two pairs that last a month where previously they only bought one; or by buying eight pairs which wear out after a week. The consumer appears much better off in this case, but it is an improvement that is more apparent than real.

In principle these two methods of increasing consumption are not mutually exclusive and in practice both occur together. But in so far as the latter is growing in importance and serves the interests of capital more than the former it must be looked at more closely. The relevant concept in this context is the *period of consumption*. Production, we have seen, takes place in time and its analysis must take account of the period of production. Similarly consumption has its temporal dimension and we must recognise the period of consumption, that is the time during which a commodity continues to serve as a use-value and satisfies some human need or requirement. Furthermore the duration of this period is the nearest we can get to a measure of use-value, for it makes sense to say, other things being equal, that the longer a commodity fulfils its material functions the greater is its use-value. A pair of tights that lasts for two weeks can be said in this way to have twice as much use-value as a pair that lasts only one week; and a car that runs for five years has only one third of the use-value of one with identical specifications that runs for fifteen years.

At the same time, it does not follow that these differences in use-value are matched by similar differences in value, for there is no in-built reason why a commodity that lasts twice as long as another which serves the same purpose, should require twice as much labour, direct and indirect, to make. In fact, it often requires considerable effort to build obsolescence into a product. In addition there are other ways of shortening the useful life of a commodity than material frailty. Changes in fashion are far and away the most important, and many commodities are discarded long before their useful life is at an end materially because they are no longer in style. In other words, an increase in the value of consumption does not necessarily mean an increase in use-value. The real benefits that capital bestows with the one hand it takes away with the other.

The advantages, to capital, of accelerated depreciation and a reduction in quality and durability are plain and easy to understand. Given the fact that the intensification of labour demands an increase in the value of wages and consumption, capital has two choices. The first is to produce high-quality goods and extend the range of production to keep pace with increasing consumption: the other is reduce use-value relative to value so that the range of new goods needs to be extended relatively more slowly. Adopting the latter course saves on the costs of real renovations and development: it is much cheaper to carry out superficial changes that give all the impression of novelty and in addition help to accelerate depreciation. It also has the effect of confusing the nature of exploitation and making it appear a feature of consumption rather than production. This confusion is aided by the fact that reductions in quality are experienced by all sections of society not just the working class and can therefore be easily defined as a 'social problem' and not seen in class terms. Middle class protest in recent years, the formation of consumer protection groups and even legislation show not only how widely the effects of reduced quality are experienced, but more important how effectively the bourgeoisie can absorb working class opposition. Under the stifling blanket of middle class moralism the real issue is clouded. The real struggle against reduced quality that is carried on by the workers who oppose the inhuman conditions of intensified labour in factories where mass production takes place is turned into a fashionable discussion of the relative merits of one brand of good compared with another.

In this connection the car industry is of supreme importance. Here superficial changes and accelerated depreciation have been developed to a fine art and public outrage against the irresponsibility of manufacturers has been orchestrated into a self-righteous crescendo. Endless discussion about the advantages and disadvantages of different models is encouraged to replace the real criticism of the conditions under which *all* cars are produced. Defects in the quality of the product are seen in terms of moral lapse on the part of individual producers, and not as part of the general process of capitalist development whereby quality is continuously subordinated to quantity in an endless effort to speed up production and increase the rate of exploitation and accumulation. Pollution, urban decay and all the other problems brought about by the consumption of cars are unquestionably aspects of the real absurdity of capitalist production, but the real significance of the car as the quintessence of capitalism lies in its mode of production rather than in its mode of consumption.

2. *Fordism*

This is the case not simply for the general reason that the forces that ultimately determine the nature of society are located in the sphere of production, not the sphere of consumption; but because the production of cars, in particular, has played a leading role in the reorganisation of production in this century. It was the motor industry that pioneered modern methods of mass production, and the introduction of the conveyor-belt by Ford shortly before the First World War was recognised even by contemporaries as a decisive new development. 'The most interesting metal working establishment in the world' was how two of his admirers described his new factory in 1915, and the effectiveness of this new technology as a means of raising the rate of exploitation by increasing both the productivity and intensity of labour, needs no rehearsal now. 'Every piece of work in the shop moves', said Ford himself, perhaps not realising that this movement was the movement of value and that his new methods allowed capital to express itself more fully than any other – value in motion! On the other hand his instinctive knowledge about the nature of exploitation should not be underestimated: no better insight into the mechanics of intensification can be found than his idea that 'the man must have every second necessary, but not a single unnecessary second'.[2]

The innovations pioneered by Ford were not merely technical and they had implications that stretched far beyond the economic realm. The process of production in capitalist society is a process of exploitation which has historically required overt social expression. Not only must the direct producers be denied

[2] Huw Benyon, *Working for Ford* (London: Penguin Books, 1973), p. 19.

all independent access to the means of production and forced to become wage-labourers in order to acquire their means of subsistence, but the process of production has been organised, wherever possible, in a way that consolidates this oppression. Capital must always attempt to combine the technical requirements of sophisticated production and the social imperative to control the direct producers at the moment of their exploitation. The particular conditions prevailing in Detroit before the First World War gave a special impetus to innovations that could secure this double goal. The place was something of a frontier town with a disorderly labour-force consisting of many immigrant workers few of whom had the skills necessary for metal production as it was organised at that time. Many could not even speak English, but Ford organised his plant in such a way that the only word they needed to know was 'wage'. He developed a system of production which is unparalleled as a method of discipling workers and mobilising a mass of unskilled labour for the production of a technically sophisticated commodity. The detailed breakdown in the division of labour which the conveyor-belt presupposes and enforces demands little more from the worker than his capacity for effort; it empties work of its human content and makes abstract labour a living reality.[3] For this reason, alone, the innovations in Detroit had a general significance for the development of capitalism on a world scale. At the same time although local conditions made Detroit an ideal centre for a major capitalist breakthrough, the development of modern mass production was never a local affair even at its inception.

    [3] 'This economic relation – the character which capitalist and worker have as the extremes of a single relation of production – therefore develops more purely and adequately in proportion as labour loses all the characteristics of art; as its particular skill becomes more and more abstract and irrelevant, and as it becomes more and more a *purely abstract activity*, a purely mechanical activity, hence indifferent to its particular form; a merely formal activity, or, what is the same, a merely material activity, activity pure and simple, regardless of its form' (Marx, *Grundrisse*, p. 297). The growth of industrial sociology and psychology must be understood in this context. Freed from any meaningful work, all that ties the abstract worker to society is the compulsion to work – i.e. capital. The policy of work reorganisation on the principle of job enrichment is an attempt to reverse the historic trend of accumulation and provide new subjective means to bind the worker to the conditions of his exploitation.

The years before and after the First World War were a period of intensified class struggle, which, although not tightly co-ordinated and organised between different countries, were nevertheless international in their scope. The unsuccessful Russian Revolution of 1905 was echoed in a wave of violent strikes throughout Europe and North America. In 1904 the first general strike took place in Italy; a miners strike that shook the Ruhr in 1905 followed two earlier strikes by textile and paper workers in 1903 and 1904. A wave of strikes in the United States starting in 1901 culminated in the establishment of the International Workers of the World (the I.W.W. or *Wobblies*) in 1905. Britain was similarly affected and 1906 saw the firm establishment of the Labour Party in Parliament. The Soviet Revolution of 1917 was every bit as much a part of an international working class movement and the confidence of its leaders that it was merely a prelude to a wider revolution throughout Europe, at first supported by revolutionary struggles in Germany and Italy, was matched everywhere by an anxiety among the ruling classes.[4] The ideological spearhead of this revolution surge was the *workers' council* or *soviet* – the extrapolation into the sphere of politics of workers' control and self-management in the sphere of production. Despite its articulation into a vanguard party struggling outside the factories, the worker in his role of producer was the real subject of this phase of struggle.

But for the worker to accept this definition, the process of production must allow him to identify with his work in some meaningful way. It must have some actual content that engages his faculties in a way that offers some possibility for self-realisation. The relationship between the nature of work and the workers' situation in the process of production on the one hand, and his political adherences on the other is not exact. Nevertheless the two correspond closely. In a major article which explores this relationship in the context of the German working class movement at the close of the First World War, Sergio Bologna reaches the following conclusion:

[4] See Sergio Bologna, 'Class Composition and the Theory of the Party at the Origin of the Workers-Council Movement', *Telos*, No. 13 (Fall, 1972), pp. 3–27, and Guido Baldi, 'Theses on Mass Worker and Social Capital', *Radical America*, vol. 6, No. 3 (May–June, 1972), pp. 3–21.

It is no mere coincidence that the worker-councils movement acquired the most marked political and managerial characteristics precisely in those three regions where the machine tool, electromechanic and optical industries were most concentrated, i.e. where highly specialised workers were predominant within the overall labour force. These highly specialised workers of the machine and tool industry with a high level of professional ability, engaged in precision work, perfectly familiar with tools (both manual and mechanical) and working alongside technicians and engineers in modifying the working process, were *materially* most susceptible to a political-organisational project such as the workers-councils, i.e. workers' self-management of production. The concept of workers' self-management could not have had such a wide appeal in the German workers-council movement without a labour-force inextricably linked to the technology of the working process, with high professional values and naturally inclined to stress their function as 'producers'. The concept of self-management pictured the worker as an autonomous producer and the factory's labour-power as self-sufficient.[5]

It was precisely this type of worker that Fordism dispensed with. The *labour aristocracy* was replaced by the *mass worker* whose response to work was no longer pride but boredom and rejection. In this way the material basis of a whole phase revolutionary struggle was undermined. In Bologna's words:

Ford's innovations did not amount to mere qualitative changes of machinery, but, in the long run, they meant the progressive extinction of the type of worker bound to the machine, to the factory, and to the craft. The highly skilled worker of the machine-tool industry was to give way to the unskilled, uprooted, highly mobile and inter-changeable modern assembly line worker. Thus, it is important to keep in mind that before the German 'labour-aristocracy' became the revolutionary vanguard, before it underwent the acid test, it had been objectively doomed to extinction by the capitalist vanguards.[6]

[5] Bologna, 'Class Composition', pp. 5–6.
[6] Ibid., p. 7.

The establishment of modern mass production at Detroit before the First World War was thus much more than a response to local labour conditions; much more, even, than a brilliant technical initiative to increase the productivity and intensity of labour in keeping with the imperatives of accumulation. It was nothing less than the economic basis for a political riposte to a massive working class assault, and not only did it secure its immediate tactical objectives, but also laid the economic foundations for a political strategy that has served capital successfully for more than half a century.

8. Crisis and Recomposition

'No social order is ever destroyed', wrote Marx in 1859, 'before all the productive forces for which it is sufficient have been developed, and new superior relations of production never replaced older ones before the material conditions for their existence have matured within the framework of the old society.'[1] By these criteria no social order can enter a *general crisis* until it has realised its full historical potential and is no longer able to contain the social and material developments which it sets in motion. Thus capitalism survives so long as it can revolutionise and socialise production. Its development has been punctuated by periods of crisis when a particular line of advance has been blocked, but so far capital has been able to turn these crises to its own advantage. It has restricted their impact and succeeded in turning them into *crises of recomposition*, whereby the forces that appear to threaten the very existence of the capitalist mode of production become the basis for a new phase of development.

1. Crisis

The most recent crisis of capitalism came this century between the two world wars at a time when its capacities to innovate were far from used up. The Ford experiment before the First World War is clear proof that its ability to awaken the 'productive forces that slumbered in the lap of social labour' and reorganise the relations of production at their roots, was far from exhausted. As a result, working class opposition though intense, perhaps more intense and more effectively organised than ever before, was unable to gain any stategic autonomy and dictate the terms and terrain of struggle. Its main attack, spearheaded by the worker in his role as producer, was conducted on ground that the advance-guard of capital had already surpassed and was generally preparing to abandon. Its project for socialism centring on a programme of nationalisa-

[1] Marx, *The Critique of Political Economy*, p. 21.

tion and planning already formed part of advanced capitalist strategy and constituted no fundamental threat. On the contrary, the working class offensive during this period was directed in the main against the more backward sectors of capital and for this reason lost not only its revolutionary edge but offered itself as a motor of capitalist renovation. Revolutionary socialism sank into reformist social democracy where it was swamped by Keynesianism.

The issue of unemployment reveals this more fully than any other. In recent years it has become the practice to treat the level of employment as an indicator of capitalist success, and the high unemployment of the inter-war period is seen as unambiguous evidence of a crisis. But for whom was it a crisis? There are no economic imperatives for capital to create full employment as the situation in the underdeveloped world shows beyond dispute. This does not mean that unemployment in the advanced capitalist countries before the last war was the result of the same forces that now bring it about in so many underdeveloped countries. But it does show that unemployment does not threaten capital in itself. On the other hand it always weakens the working class because of its immediate and total dependence on wage-labour. In fact, unemployment is invariably a greater crisis for labour than capital and the depressions that periodically interrupted accumulation before 1945 unfailingly redounded to the advantage of capital. Depression demonstrates the absurdity of capitalist production more vividly than anything else – poverty on the one hand; rotting stocks, unused equipment and idle men, on the other: but, it does not follow that it is a period when the balance of class power swings away from capital. On the contrary, slumps have been periods of capitalist renovation: the weakest firms collapse, aiding the process of concentration and centralisation; equipment hastily installed during the boom is realistically revalued; and new branches of production can be expanded while unemployment weakens working class opposition. The depression in Britain in the 1930s, for example, was the occasion of much renovation and structural change in industry. Areas of production where working class resistance was strong such as coal, steel, railways and the docks, were run down and new industries, such as chemical and electrical engineering, which employed labour in a different kind of way, were expanded rapidly. In the midst of the 'crisis' Ford moved to Dagenham.

Having said this, it must be recognised that the political significance of unemployment varies from one situation to the next, and that capital is not always at equal liberty to deploy it against labour. In regimes of consensus politics such as have prevailed in the developed countries since the end of the last war, unemployment is a strategy that capital must forsake in the interests of political stability. Advanced thinkers between the wars were well aware of this, though they considered the issue from the other side, perceiving that full employment could not only outmanœuvre working class opposition but actually aid the incorporation of the working class and its institutions into the capitalist project.

> Democracy [wrote Harold Macmillan in 1938, meaning, of course, capitalism] can live only so long as it is able to cope satisfactorily with the problems of social life. While it is able to deal with these problems, and secure for its people the satisfaction of their reasonable demands, it will retain the vigorous support sufficient for its defence.[2]

Although the organisational forms through which working class struggle was expressed in the thirties, trade unions and parliamentary parties, were unable to issue a decisive challenge to capital, they represented a political force which capital could not ignore. At the same time, precisely because they posed no revolutionary threat, they appeared to the advance guards of the capitalist class not as deadly enemies but as potential partners in a far-sweeping and broadly based programme for reshaping the nineteenth-century capitalist order. In Britain, Keynes believed that the Liberal Party could provide the organisational framework for the new consensus, and although this particular aspiration was not realised, his general political insight was fully vindicated. Just after the General Strike, and long before he achieved world fame with the *General Theory*, he advised the Liberal Party to purge itself of those of its members 'who believe with Mr. Winston Churchill . . . that the coming

---

[2] Harold Macmillan, *The Middle Way*, 1st ed., 1938 (London: Macmillan, 1966), p. 375.

political struggle (in Britain) is best described as capitalism versus socialism'.[3] But as Keynes realised full well the separation of working class organisations from any revolutionary programme, and their incorporation into the new capitalist project, required a commitment to full employment. In part this was a concessionary bargaining-counter. But more importantly working class organisations such as trade unions and social democratic parties with roots in the labour movement can only participate actively in the capitalist state; while retaining their hold over the working class, if some of the real demands of this class are satisfied. Keynes was also aware that the implementation of this strategy would involve a shift to a 'high-wage economy' though it took him a further ten years to prove the point academically in the *General Theory*. Ford, incidentally, had anticipated this as early as 1914 when he increased the daily wage in his factory from $2·30 to $5·00. What perhaps Keynes would have been reluctant to admit was that the success of the new strategy after the Second World War would have been less but for the chastening effects on the working class of large-scale unemployment in the twenties and thirties.

While full employment cut the ground from under the feet of the revolutionary movement on the one side, the means proposed for its implementation – state intervention – were hardly less effective on the other. On this issue Keynes was never less than ambiguous. Realising full well that *laissez-faire* as an ideology and practice could no longer serve the interests of capitalism which 'wisely managed, can probably be made more efficient for attaining economic ends than any alternative system in sight', he defined the problem as the need 'to work out a social organisation which shall be as efficient as possible without offending our notions of a satisfactory way of life'.[4] He recognised the necessity of state intervention as an essential element in this new 'social organisation' but could never repudiate the supposed advantages of the market as a mechanism of social distribution. With deep roots in English political culture and a profound faith in the scientific merits of neo-

---

[3] J. M. Keynes, *Collected Works*, vol. IX (London: Macmillan, 1972), p. 310.

[4] Ibid., p. 294.

classical economics, which he never lost despite the many criticisms he made of it,[5] Keynes was ultimately unable to see beyond the boundaries of private property in the way that many subsequent Keynesians have managed. Thus ironically in Western Europe, though not the United States, it was those very socialist parties that Keynes wished to defeat with a refurbished liberalism, that really seized his ideas and turned them into an effective political force.

This success of capital, its ability not only to ride the crisis of the inter-war period, but use it as a basis for a far-sweeping recomposition, should not blind us to its intensity, or even less to its pervasiveness. For the crisis of the inter-war period overwhelmed the whole capitalist world to an unprecedented degree. It was a genuinely international crisis engulfing both developed and underdeveloped countries alike, illustrating more vividly than any other single event, the extent to which capital had unified the world economy by the beginning of the twentieth century.

Since 1850, when industrial capital asserted its dominance over merchant capital and made it its agent in the underdeveloped world, developments in the two parts of the capitalist world were closely tied to each other. The pattern of economic change in the underdeveloped countries was determined by the metropolitan powers. Not only was the structure of material production and consumption subordinated to the requirements of industrial capital, but the periodic booms and slumps which marked the progress of accumulation in the developed countries were transmitted overseas. Yet the underdeveloped countries were never simply satellites with no autonomy whatsoever. The manner of their subordination to industrial capital was always decisively influenced by local conditions and varied from one country and territory to another. Moreover the structure of the international economy was subject to its own specific contradictions, over which industrial capital was never able to exer-

---

[5] At the end of the *General Theory*, Keynes made a desperate effort to reconcile his work with traditional neo-classicism. 'I see no reason to suppose that the existing system seriously misemploys the factors of production that are in use . . . When 9,000,000 men are employed out of 10,000,000 willing and able to work, there is no evidence that the labour of these 9,000,000 men is misdirected' (J. M. Keynes, *The General Theory of Employment, Interest and Money* (London: Macmillan, 1960), p. 379).

cise total control. Nor were these contradictions a simple projection of developments in the metropolitan powers, and the
crisis of the international economy in the inter-war period was
more than a simple reflection of the crisis of recomposition in
the developed world. It had its own autonomous sources and
played an active role in precipitating this recomposition. This
was particularly true in Britain which at the centre of world
economy was both meeting point and transmitter of what can
be thought of, initially, at least, as two crises.

Between 1850 and the reorganisation of the world economy
after the Second World War, economic relations between
industrial capital in the developed countries and producers in
the underdeveloped world were mediated by merchant capital.
But merchant capital was always in a vulnerable position.
Squeezed by industrial capital in the developed countries and
unable to reorganise production in the underdeveloped world,
its rate of profit was always subject to pressures that ultimately
it was unable to withstand. These pressures asserted themselves
long before the depression of the early thirties reduced the
demand for primary commodities in the developed world; and
the international economic order in which merchant capital
played a central part was already in a state of profound crisis
by the end of the First World War.

The British were fully aware of the dangers in this situation,
particularly for the home economy. The issue was raised
obliquely as a question of the gold standard and during the
early twenties a fierce controversy raged about merits of this
way of organising international finance and whether it should
be restored. Conservative opinion held that a return to gold was
essential to the re-establishment of 'normal' economic conditions as the gold standard provided an automatic mechanism
whereby balance of payments disequilibria could be corrected
in the most effective way and with the minimum amount of
disruption. Its opponents, such as Keynes, denied this strongly,
claiming that the international balance could only be achieved
through massive unemployment and futile efforts to force down
the level of wages. More recent research, while accepting the
Keynesian diagnosis in general terms, has shown that whatever
stability was achieved under the gold standard from the 1880s
down to 1914, depended upon the role played by the vast

amount of British investment overseas, particularly in the underdeveloped world, which acted as a cushion, so to speak, absorbing most of the shocks to which the structure was prone. This investment, however, was not planned with stabilisation in mind; most of it was directed into railway construction to serve the trade which merchant capital was finding less and less profitable. It could therefore not continue indefinitely on the scale that stabilisation required. Not only was there no longer the same incentive to expand trade fast enough to absorb large amounts of capital, but the nature of the projects it financed, like railways, was such that once built relatively little further expansion is required. The real basis of the international monetary economy was thus crumbling long before it was overtaken by chaos in the early thirties and abandoned for good and all. The conservative desire in Britain in the twenties to return to normal pre-war conditions was never more than a pipedream – or a justification for the fierce attack on living standards that provoked the working class into an abortive general strike. In the end the depression of the thirties marked the point of no return and finally shattered all hopes for a reconstruction of the old order. It was also the moment in which all the separate strands of the capitalist crisis converged to define both the nature and the scope of the recomposition that was required.

2. *Recomposition*

Although it was a vast social process the recomposition of capital after 1945 can be expressed in terms of two individuals and their work – Ford and Keynes. Their relationship is like that of the car to the road: the one made by private capital with dramatically new methods of production; the other constructed by the state according to new principles of political economy. Ford prepared the real basis for the new phase of development; Keynes blue-printed the social institutions in which it could operate. Representing different sections of the capitalist class their perspectives on the 'economic problem' were quite different. Ford started with production and the factory; Keynes adopted a more general perspective. Nevertheless on one fundamental question they held a common position – wages. Ford's ideas were crude and to the point:

If we can distribute high wages [he wrote in 1922], then that money is going to be spent and it will serve to make store-keepers and distributors and manufacturers in other lines more prosperous and this prosperity will be reflected in our sales. Country-wide high wages spell country-wide prosperity . . . [6]

Keynes was more circumspect and did not summarise his position in the same succinct way. Yet his outlook was fundamentally the same as that of Ford and this statement could be easily mistaken as a rough description of the *multiplier* which was one of the pivotal concepts employed in the *General Theory*. A central theme in Keynes's criticisms of government policy in the twenties was his attack on the attempt to reduce real wages directly – a theme that is taken up right at the start of the *General Theory* itself.

. . . the contention [he states] that the unemployment that characterises a depression is due to a refusal by labour to accept a reduction in money wages is not clearly supported by the facts. [7]

Of course, neither Ford nor Keynes believed that problems could be solved simply by raising wages. Their class instincts kept them clear of this error.

. . . higher wages must be paid for by higher production [said Ford]. Paying higher wages and lowering production is starting down the incline towards dull business. [8]

The need for high wages, which both men appreciated in their different ways, arose from the growth in the productivity and intensity of labour, and the orientation of the leading branches of industrial production towards commodities for the consumer market. Ford's appreciation of this need was that of the hard-headed businessman who wished to see more money in the hands of his potential customers while recognising that a better-paid worker was more productive and therefore more profitable to employ. Keynes interpreted the wages question in

[6] Ford, *My Life and Work*, p. 124.
[7] Keynes, *General Theory*, p. 9.
[8] Ford, *My Life and Work*, p. 125.

much broader terms and he was one of the few people who realised that a shift to a high-wage economy, imminent in the productive changes that Ford had initiated, could not be effected without far-sweeping reforms in the institutional framework of the capitalist economy, internationally as well as nationally.

The international ramifications of wages policy were particularly apparent in Britain in the 1920s where national and international issues were inseparable, and any proposal to reorganise the structure of wages in line with the development of production led to the inescapable conclusion that capitalism must be reorganised on a world scale. This has been fully demonstrated by the changes that took place after the last war. In all the developed countries governments rejected a strategy of direct wage cuts and committed themselves more or less formally to full employment. Later, this evolved into policies of economic growth fostered through various types of state intervention such as nationalisation, incomes policy and planning. But as Keynes realised full well this strategy could not have been successful without new organisations being set up to replace the gold standard and arrange international trade, finance and investment in a way that would reinforce these domestic policies. This involved political as well as economic initiatives.

The collapse of the gold standard spelt the end of a highly integrated structure of political ties that bound the underdeveloped world to the developed countries for more than half a century. Its most dramatic victim was the colonial system and the vast European empires of the nineteenth century were swept away in the forties and fifties as one colony after another gained formal independence. Three forces combined to bring this particular development about. First, the rise of nationalism in the underdeveloped world itself; second, pressure from the United States to get an 'open door' into formerly protected markets; and third, the realisation in advanced capitalist circles within the colonial powers themselves that the old system was doomed and that their own long-term interests could only be safeguarded by a new initiative.

In the period immediately after the Second World War these changes appeared more fundamental than they have subsequently turned out to be, partly because the cold war context in which they took place made the nationalist movements in the underdeveloped world appear more revolutionary than in fact they were. But as time passed, it became manifestly clear that in most parts of the world nationalism was organised as mass movements directed against a particular set of political and economic ties with the advanced capitalist world, and not as class movements dedicated to the overthrow of capitalism itself. It is true that in China the nationalist and revolutionary movements merged into one, and China was able to escape the fetters of the world capitalist order. But in most other places the nationalist movement was a coalition firmly under the control of national capitalist interests whose political goal was to strengthen their position *vis-à-vis* international capital – a goal whose strategic horizons fall far short of being revolutionary. The widespread adoption of revolutionary phraseology only disguised the political limits of nationalism. In many colonies the main plank in the independence movement was securing for local personnel jobs that had previously been held by expatriates. Elsewhere determined efforts were made to seize control of foreign capital, but generally these were restricted to merchant capital whose profitability was already depleted, and whose owners were, in many cases, glad to get it off their hands. Nationalisation with generous compensation satisfied both parties, allowing the one to adopt a radical posture and the other to unload an asset whose value was in decline. Fundamental capitalist interests were not threatened: in fact, nationalisation frequently aided recomposition, by providing funds for new types of investment. Except in very rare cases productive capital was not attacked and the most radical governments in the underdeveloped world always insisted that they would welcome foreign capital 'of the right sort'.

In this way they took the lead in opening the way for industrial capitalism. Just as the social democratic movement in Europe was incorporated into the strategy of capitalist renovation in the developed countries, so the nationalist movements promoted it in the underdeveloped world. For a fleeting moment at the end of the fifties they seemed to stake out an independent position for themselves around the slogan of non-alignment, but this possibility vanished almost as quickly as it appeared. The failure of seventy-six underdeveloped countries to win any major concessions from the developed countries at the first meeting of the United Nations Conference on Trade and Development in 1964, showed exactly where the balance of power lay.

Ironically the demands made by the secretariat of UNCTAD, which the underdeveloped countries supported unanimously, were perfectly consistent with the long-term interests of industrial capital and their failure to win support from the developed countries can only be explained in terms of a regressive anxiety about the dangers of communism. For what the UNCTAD wanted was a liberalisation of trade restrictions to encourage exports from the underdeveloped countries, particularly in the field of light manufactures. It envisaged a new global division of labour in which the underdeveloped countries would take over lines of manufacturing no longer profitable in the developed countries, leaving capital in these countries free to move into those branches of industry that had been pioneered before the Second World War. In other words, the main drive for the recomposition of capital came from the underdeveloped countries themselves.[9]

The ideological framework which united these apparently disparate forces was provided by the concepts of development and underdevelopment, which replaced the former colonial dichotomy of barbarism and civilisation. In the underdeveloped world they were generally understood in their structuralist sense while capital in the West tended to favour the more orthodox definitions associated with the theory of original underdevelopment. In practice, however, this difference amounted to very little, for whatever theoretical interpretation was given to the concept of underdevelopment, development in practice always meant the development of industrial capitalism. Yet it is precisely here that the new order is faltering, and proving itself unable to satisfy even its own criteria. The idea of development has always implied reproducing in the under-

---

[9] See Raul Prebisch, *Towards a New Trade Policy for Development* (New York: United Nations, 1964). A succinct summary of the report and voting pattern of various countries is contained in Harry G. Johnson, *Economic Policies towards Less Developed Countries* (London: George Allen and Unwin, 1967), pp. 251–4.

developed countries, the type of affluence experienced in the developed world. But the logic of accumulation at this stage in the world history of capitalism rules this out.

As the turnover of capital increases so history itself speeds up. Whereas an initiative in the nineteenth century could prove viable for nearly a hundred years, it now exhausts its possibilities in less than half that time. The measures that capital once used to out-manœuvre labour are turned against it with unprecedented speed. Capital must now change the terms of confrontation more rapidly than ever before; moreover the scope of the recompositions it must undertake increases while its room for manœuvre is steadily diminished. Every move that capital makes is determined by the requirements of accumulation which demands mot only a greater socialisation of production but a greater socialisation of capital itself. Its last major recomposition, conceived between the wars and executed after 1945, was a massive step forward. The new methods of production pioneered by Ford greatly accelerated the concentration and centralisation of capital; the new role of the state blue-printed by Keynes provided the organisational framework for social capital as such. Within this framework capital was able not only to articulate a conscious programme for its own accumulation; but even, to the extent that it out-flanked early revolutionary movements and incorporated key working class institutions into the apparatus of the state, it has planned the class struggle itself. But now this plan is faltering not only on the limitations of industrialisation in the underdeveloped world, but in the developed countries themselves.[10]

[10] The socialisation of capital internationally has added a new dimension to the link between development and underdevelopment. In addition to the previous ties of trade and investment, there is now the migrant worker who, unable to find employment in his own country or region, is drawn to the metropolitan centres. Moreover many of these workers are finding their way into the most advanced centres of capitalist production, the car industry, where they make up a sizeable proportion of the labour force – Southern Italians in Turin, Turks in Hamburg, Algerians at Billancourt, Indians and West Indians in Dagenham and Langley, and Blacks in Detroit. The modern mass worker who has led some of the most significant struggles against capital in recent years is very often a worker from the underdeveloped world.

3. Democracy and repression

Inflation is the economic strategy of consensus. Since 1945 the incorporation of the trade union movement and social democracy has pre-empted traditional measures of controlling wages like unemployment and direct cuts. Experience in the twenties had already taught the advance-guards of the capitalist class that these measures were fraught with danger and no longer corresponded to real requirements of capital. New methods were required that recognised the power of working class organisations but nevertheless could keep them in check: methods which conceded the right of the trade union movement to fight for higher living standards but could simultaneously be used to control wages. They were discovered in the strategy of inflation whereby excessive gains won by the working class in the sphere of production could be confiscated by rising prices in the sphere of consumption.

> Whilst workers will usually resist a reduction in money wages [wrote Keynes in the *General Theory*], it is not their practice to withdraw their labour whenever there is a rise in the price of wage-goods.[11]

But working class practice changes and the secrets of inflation are not that difficult to fathom. Even without compulsory education there are few workers unable to calculate that a 3 per cent price rise halves the purchasing power of 6 per cent increase in wages. Those incapable of this sum were anyway continually informed by the government that inflation reduced real wages in the hope that this knowledge would keep claims in check. But working class logic is not as subtle as that of the economists, and Keynes's maxim that workers do not respond to rising prices works in two directions. While it is true 'that no trade union would dream of striking on every occasion of a rise in the cost of living',[12] it is no less the case that no trade union would dream of reducing a wage claim because prices go up. Inflation is a game that two can play and once the working class had learnt the rules by the end of the fifties it discovered it had certain natural advantages.

---

[11] Keynes, *General Theory*, p. 9.
[12] Ibid., p. 15.

Of all the strategies that capital has yet evolved inflation demands greater social coherence than any other: it is *par excellence* a strategy of social capital. If individual firms do not toe the line problems soon arise. A firm that is prepared to concede higher wages to its workers because productivity is rising faster than the national average, or market conditions allow it to more than recoup its losses, opens a gap in the capitalist lines which labour will be quick to exploit. In most of the developed countries conditions in the car industry were such that firms involved in this branch of production were often willing to increase wages more than capital in other branches of production, and so set a target for workers throughout the whole economy. Thus by the late sixties governments throughout the developed world were forced to implement some form of incomes policy upon individual firms in the hope that by disciplining capital they would be able to discipline labour. Social capital as an organised force began to assert its power directly over the individual capitalist in one of the most important areas of enterprise.[13]

At first this seemed to open the possibility for a yet deeper incorporation of the working class into the capitalist project and a further strengthening of the structure of consensus politics. For if the state were prepared to act against individual capitalists, its claim to neutrality between capital and labour was more clearly vindicated than ever, and the trade unions could accept its invitation to participate directly in the planning of the economy without any qualms of conscience. But trade unions and the working class are quite different. The worker is a worker first and a trade unionist second, and he will only follow his union's lead as long as it corresponds to his real interests as a worker. The more direct involvement of the trade unions in the making and implementation of economic policy, which first

[13] The need for coherence at the level of social capital applies internationally as well as nationally, for different rates of inflation among countries by creating balance of payments problems destabilise the organisation of international finance and therefore produce difficulties for all countries, creditors and debtors alike. The attempts to reform the international monetary system would be better understood if they were seen less in technical terms and more as an attempt by capital to develop a global organisation for the articulation and implementation of an international wages policy.

appeared as a major stride to the corporate state, led, paradoxically, to a serious rupture in the fabric of consensus politics. The chief reason for this is the ambiguous role that consensus politics forces upon the trade unions.

Trade unions are first and foremost working class organisations and can only exist as an effective political force so long as they represent the real interests of the working class. It is not necessary for them to be revolutionary, but they must, at least, have the appearance of autonomy. Once they are drawn directly into the framework of the state this appearance is threatened, particularly if the outcome of high-level negotiations is a moderation of wage claims. Like the tribal chiefs through whom colonial governments exercised indirect rule, they become the focal point of social contradictions. The more they become bound into the apparatus of state and the more the state attempts to reinforce their position *vis-à-vis* the working class by administrative and legislative dictat, the more their lack of automony is exposed, and their power in and over the working class weakened. Drawn first one way and then the other, a ploy they have adopted in many countries is to call one-day national strikes which improve their negotiating position with capital and prove to the working class that they are still an independent and radical force. But as the working class comes to appreciate these stage-managed dramas for what they really are, and learns that locally organised stoppages are far more effective means of winning real wage increases, the situation of the trade unions is made more precarious. Unable to struggle effectively in the national arena the working class deserts its representatives in the consensus and turns to guerrilla warfare. Throughout the developed world capital is already articulating a twofold response. On the one hand it is trying to strengthen the consensus by reforms that permit the workers greater participation at all levels of the capitalist project; on the other, it is evolving novel methods to discipline dissidents and restrict the development of new autonomous working-class organisations. Its plan for democratic repression is typified by the modern soldier who not only shoots straight but has also mastered the rudiments of sociology.

In the underdeveloped world consensus politics has proved impossible. The efforts to establish two-party systems in the late colonial period were never more than half-hearted and few of the constitutions set up by the departing colonial powers survived more than five years after independence. Political scientists who were full of praise for democracy in 1960, had no sooner adjusted themselves to one-party states by 1965 when they were forced to explain that military take-overs might not be so bad as they appear. The immediate reason for the failure of consensus politics in the underdeveloped world was the existence of high levels of unemployment that made repression essential for the survival of the state. At a more profound level it serves the interests of capital in the developed countries. Just as the poverty of the underdeveloped world throws the affluence of the developed countries into sharp relief, so open repression makes democratic repression look like true freedom. Moreover the underdeveloped world is an ideal laboratory for capitalist experimentation. Just as the Nazis were able to test the *Luftwaffe* in Spain, and the Russians and Americans can compare their armaments in Vietnam and the Middle East, so new methods of controlling civilian populations can be tried out in relatively quiet back-waters. In their colonies around the world the British perfected a form of judicial-administrative dictatorship far more advanced than any that has existed in the modern world. In the sphere of production the developed countries are more advanced; in the development of methods of open repression the underdeveloped world points the way forward. In this sense the country that is less developed industrially only shows, to the more developed, the image of its own future.

List of Works Cited

Ed. A. N. Agarwala and S. P. Singh, *The Economics of Underdevelopment* (London: Oxford University Press, 1958).

Guido Baldi, 'Theses on the Mass Worker and Social Capital', *Radical America*, vol. 6, No. 3 (May–June 1972).

Paul Baran, *The Political Economy of Growth* (London: Penguin Books, 1973).

Paul Baran and Paul Sweezy, *Monopoly Capital* (London: Penguin Books, 1968).

Charles Bettelheim and Paul Sweezy, *The Transition from Capitalism to Socialism* (London and New York: Monthly Review Press, 1971).

Huw Benyon, *Working for Ford* (London: Penguin Books, 1973).

Ed. Henry Bernstein, *Underdevelopment and Development* (London: Penguin Books, 1973).

Sergio Bologna, 'Class Composition and the Theory of the Party at the Origin of the Workers-Councils Movement', *Telos*, No. 13 (Fall, 1972).

A. W. Cardinal, *The Gold Coast, 1931* (Accra: Government Printer, 1931).

E. H. Carr, *The Bolshevik Revolution*, vol. 2 (London: Macmillan, 1951; London: Penguin Books, 1971).

F. A. Clairmonte, *Economic Liberalism and Underdevelopment* (Bombay: Asia Publishing House, 1960).

Arghiri Emmanuel, *Unequal Exchange* (London: New Left Books, 1972). Also Theoretical Comments by Charles Bettelheim in appendices.

Andre Gunder Frank, *Capitalism and Underdevelopment in Latin America* (New York and London: Monthly Review Press, 1969).

—— *The Sociology of Development* (London: Pluto Press, 1971).

Henry Ford, *My Life and Work* (London: William Heinemann, 1922).

Celso Furtado, *Development and Underdevelopment* (Berkeley and Los Angeles: University of California Press, 1964).

—— *Diagnosis of the Brazilian Crisis* (Berkeley and Los Angeles: University of California Press, 1966).

J. K. Galbraith, *The New Industrial State* (London: Penguin Books, 1969).

Keith Griffin, *Underdevelopment and Spanish America* (London: George Allen and Unwin, 1969).

Harry G. Johnson, *Economic Policies towards Less Developed Countries* (London: George Allen and Unwin, 1967).

Ed. Richard Jolly, Emanuel de Kadt, Hans Singer and Fiona Wilson, *Third World Employment* (London, 1973): articles by W. Baer and M. E. Hervé, 'Employment and Industrialisation in Developing Countries'; and C. R. Frank, 'Urban Unemployment and Economic Growth in Africa'.

G. B. Kay, *The Political Economy of Colonialism in Ghana* (London: Cambridge University Press, 1972).

J. M. Keynes, *Collected Works*, vol. IX (London: Macmillan, 1972).

J. M. Keynes, *The General Theory of Employment, Interest and Money* (London: Macmillan, 1960).

Michael Kidron, *Western Capitalism since the War* (London: Penguin Books, 1970).

Charles P. Kindleberger, *Economic Development*, 2nd. ed. (New York and London: McGraw-Hill, 1965).

Ernesto Laclau, 'Imperialism in Latin America', *New Left Review*, No. 67 (May–June, 1971).

V. I. Lenin, 'Can the Bolsheviks Retain State Power?', *Selected Works*, vol. 3 (Lawrence and Wishart, 1971).

Harold Macmillan, *The Middle Way* (London: Macmillan, 1938).

Karl Marx, *A Contribution to the Critique of Political Economy* (London: Lawrence and Wishart, 1971).

—— *Grundrisse* (London: Penguin Books, 1973).

—— *Capital*, vol. 1, 3rd ed. (London: George Allen and Unwin); vols. 2 and 3 (London: Lawrence and Wishart).

—— *Theories of Surplus Value*, in 3 parts (London: Lawrence and Wishart).

—— *The Revolutions of 1848* (London: Penguin Books in association with *New Left Review*, 1973).

—— *Surveys from Exile* (London: Penguin Books in association with *New Left Review*, 1973).

Marx and Engels, *Selected Works* (London: Lawrence and Wishart).

Alfred Marshall, *Principles of Economics*, 8th ed. (London: Macmillan, 1920).

H. Myint, *The Economics of Developing Countries* (London: Hutchinson University Library, 1967).

Ed. Roger Owen and Bob Sutcliffe, *Studies in the Theory of Imperialism* (London: Longman, 1972).

Paul Prebisch, *Towards a New Trade Policy for Development* (New York: United Nations, 1964).

Robert I. Rhodes, *Imperialism and Underdevelopment* (New York and London: Monthly Review Press, 1970).

Joan Robinson, *Economic Philosophy* (London: Penguin Books, 1962).

Joan Robinson and John Eatwell, *An Introduction to Modern Economics* (London: McGraw-Hill, 1973).

W. W. Rostow, *The Stages of Economic Growth* (London: Cambridge University Press, 1960).

Adam Smith, *The Wealth of Nations*, 6th ed. (London: Methuen, 1961).

R. B. Sutcliffe, *Industry and Underdevelopment* (London and Massachusetts: Addison-Wesley Publishing Company, 1971).

Paul Sweezy, *The Theory of Capitalist Development* (New York and London: Monthly Review Press, 1968).

United Nations, *The Growth of World Industry, 1938–61* (New York, 1965).

Index